AF130753

Stephanie Theresa Bartomioli

The European Union

United Through Popular Sports

Anchor Compact

**Bartomioli, Stephanie Theresa: The European Union: United Through Popular Sports,
Hamburg, Anchor Academic Publishing 2015**
Original title of the thesis: The Simple Bare Necessities: Forging an EU-Identity Through
Popular Sports

Buch-ISBN: 978-3-95489-356-0
PDF-eBook-ISBN: 978-3-95489-856-5
Druck/Herstellung: Anchor Academic Publishing, Hamburg, 2015

Bibliografische Information der Deutschen Nationalbibliothek:
Die Deutsche Nationalbibliothek verzeichnet diese Publikation in der Deutschen
Nationalbibliografie; detaillierte bibliografische Daten sind im Internet über
http://dnb.d-nb.de abrufbar

Bibliographical Information of the German National Library:
The German National Library lists this publication in the German National Bibliography.
Detailed bibliographic data can be found at: http://dnb.d-nb.de

© Anchor Academic Publishing, ein Imprint der Diplomica® Verlag GmbH
http://www.diplom.de, Hamburg 2015
Printed in Germany

TABLE OF CONTENTS

Preface: An EU masterpiece at the Olympics

"Look, mommy, this French lady runs the same way we do. French people do have the same sports as we do, don't they?" (Willem, 4 years old)

My son shared me this remarkably recondite observation while watching a women's sprint heat at the Olympics 2012 in London unsheathing the universally uniting quality of sport, a characteristic recognizable even to a small child. Its profound impact on politics, society and economy can hardly be grasped.

In the Olympic Games the world has a peaceful, representative, and global event which celebrates the multitude of sports around the world and espouses the spirit of competition through a well-mannered rivalry for medals between the nations. The European Union did not only host these marvelous competitions but its athletes' performances have been a source of pride for all people of the Union. Thus, the members of the European Union achieved an incredible feat this past Olympics by winning more medals than the United States of America and China combined.[1] Although the European Union is not officially evaluated, the perception of the European Union as an athletic social and political entity raises the discussion on a mutually acknowledged EU-identity to a new level.[2] Why has the EU traditionally been perceived in such a way under these favorable circumstances that people were cheering for *us*, the Europeans?

The European Union is a vivid and globally unique sample of successful and distinctive supranational integration[3]. It is a safe, wealthy, appealing and powerful business location[4] whose success has forged the foundation of a potential identity of its own. Moreover, the EU can rely on "societies that are […] based on the European political and cultural tradition"[5] all over the world and thus, a projective identity would not differ substantially from existing nation-state identities and thence not cause discrepancy. Europe has succeeded in sharing sovereignty and envisaging commonly approved solutions for modern problems.[6] Its political union

---

[1] Cf. http://www.medaillenspiegel.eu

[2] Despite this success, the expectation to send one EU team to the next Olympics to Rio is naïve. Moreover, ne has to take into consideration that this team would hardly be able to repeat since various reasons (IOC reglement referring to the number of athletes, nation state pride, national sports associations, to name the most obvious ones) are opposing.

[3] Cf. **Weidenfeld**, Werner, **Turek**, Jürgen, Wie Zukunft entsteht. Größere Risiken – weniger Sicherheit – neue Chancen, München 2002, p. 178.

[4] Cf. Ibid., p. 179.

[5] **McCormick**, John, Understanding the European Union. A Concise Introduction, New York, NY 2011, p. 24.

[6] Cf. **Westerwelle**, Guido, Der Wert Europas: Vier Thesen zum Zukunftsprojekt Europa, in: integration, 2012 (2), p. 91.

"is one manifestation of that European identity"[7]. It cannot be said that a common EU-identity has been generated yet to the extent that it might be compared to nation-state identities; though hitherto integration has led to profound socialization.[8]

This study aims at responding to the question, to what extent popular sport can make a contribution to the genesis, the implementation, and the fostering of a mutually acknowledged and experienced EU-identity. With sports being the major social movement in Europe[9] – unique in its efficiency in bringing people together, a driving force for integration, bridging any kind of borders and its nonpareil ubiquity – its implementation on a European level targeting the European Union people through popular sports will sustainably and remarkably promote the idea of an EU-identity. As an example for a small but utterly profound project, the idea of a European Sports Badge (EUSB) is presented as a transnationally implementable proposal, involving and addressing EU-citizens of all nations, sexes and ages. It should be noted, though, that sports are certainly not a panacea.[10] Measures in the domain of sport can contribute to the establishment of an EU-identity, but they cannot stand alone and demand supporting actions grounded in other domains.

To describe the idea on which this project is grounded, a short historical review will introduce the topic and briefly outline actions already undertaken by the lay European Union. Secondly, present and potential future challenges will be analyzed and thus, thirdly, lead to the explanatory statement why an EU-identity is necessary. As an entitative document, this study refers to the EU White Paper on Sport. In a second step, the blueprint of a prospective EU-identity will be developed, carving out and analyzing seven components and accounting for EU-pluralism. It filters the most important components that are needed to construct a resistant EU-identity. Initially, its manifoldness and its nature will be explored. Each of the seven components shall be derived from pertinent literature. In order to not lose the essential point, the examination will be narrowed down to the EU-identity, without trying to explain any outside factors.

Subsequently, the EUSB project will be introduced. Therefore, a differentiation between the two main spheres of sport, professional sports and popular sports, shows that the official and documented emphasis of the EU on the professional sphere hitherto led to negligence and a

---

[7] **Thatcher**, Margaret, A Family of Nations, in: **Nelsen**, Brent F., **Stubb**, Alexander C-G. (Eds.), The European Union, Boulder, CO 1994, p. 51.

[8] Cf. **Göler**, Daniel, Die Grenzen des "Cost-of-Non-Europe"-Narrativs: Anmerkungen zur Sinnstiftung der Europäischen Integration, in: integration, 2012 (2), p. 134.

[9] Cf. **Tokarski**, Walter, **Steinbach**, Dirk, Spuren. Sportpolitik und Sportstrukturen in der Europäischen Union, Aachen 2001, p. 54.

[10] Cf. **Dumont**, Jacques, Le sport, vecteur d'intégration ? 1952, première tournée en Europe d'une équipe guadeloupéenne, in : **Villain-Gandossi**, Christiane (Ed.), L'Europe à la recherche de son identité, Paris 2002, p. 459.

misconceiving attitude towards mass sports so far. The EUSB targets a large audience through popular sports. The aforementioned identity blueprint will be tested by applying it to the EUSB. Moreover, favorable side effects of the implementation of the EUSB impacting on other domains will be presented. In a concluding step, the *bare necessities* of action will be expounded, taking the results of the study into consideration. The sustainability and range of small projects within the scope of identity policy has to be recognized and must lead to an increased willingness to act on the part of the EU.

1. Mapping the road

This first section is dedicated to outlining the way the European Union has covered so far, the analysis of potential obstacles that might appear on the way ahead and the presentation of the White Book on Sport as an official interpretative document.

While the idea of a European society can be traced back into the 19th century[11], it was only after World War II that the European journey truly accelerated and the institutionalization of the idea of a European entity started taking shape. Doing so, the traditional idea of nationalism has been overcome to the benefit of "regional cooperation"[12] on a European level; simultaneously fostering integration.[13] Two major positions sprouted: On the one hand, federalists held the view that the idea of nation states would be neutralized as the result of a dynamic integration, on the other hand, traditionalists were convinced that the compromises would not go beyond the economic domain.[14] As we know today, the traditionalists' position has been devitalized. At the same time, the federalists' view has not reached its true potential either.

After the end of World War II and the subsequent re-organization of the European continent, the end of the Cold War is the decisive marker on the road. The end of the bipolar world ruled off the old benchmarks and heralded a new era.[15] Not only did the European Community have to re-define its position in the new world order, it also had to find a way to justify its role. The resultant globalization process forced scholars in the domain of International Relations to shift the perspective from a nation-state dominated one[16], since the European Union is "a political experiment in taking the civilizing process beyond the nation state"[17]. The political unification of Europe is being performed on a rational level – since lasting peace can only be realized by finding answers to blazing political conflicts[18] – and leads to the dissolution of separating structures.[19] However, there has never been a concrete plan or "some eternal core idea"[20] on

---

[11] Cf. **Schäfers**, Bernhard, Sozialstruktur und sozialer Wandel in Deutschland, Stuttgart 2002, p. 311.

[12] **McCormick**, John, Understanding the European Union, p. 25.

[13] Cf. **Schmale**, Wolfgang, Geschichte und Zukunft der Europäischen Identität, Bonn 2010, p. 182.

[14] Cf. **Janz**, Louis, Die Geschichte der europäischen Einigung nach den Zweiten Weltkrieg, in: **Weidenfeld**, Werner (Ed.), Die Identität Europas, München 1985, p. 87.

[15] Cf. **Kutz**, Martin, Zentrum und Peripherie, oder: Über den Zusammenhang von kultureller und wirtschaftlicher Dynamik Europas in Geschichte und Gegenwart, in: **Kutz**, Martin, **Weyland**, Petra (Eds.), Europäische Identität? Versuch, kulturelle Aspekte eines Phantoms zu beschreiben, Bremen 2000, p. 178.

[16] Cf. **Take**, Ingo, Weltgesellschaft und Globalisierung, in: **Schieder**, Siegfried, **Spindler** Manuela (Eds.), Theorien der Internationalen Beziehungen, Opladen 2010, p. 284.

[17] **Linklater**, Andrew, A European Civilizing Process, in: **Hill**, Christopher, **Smith**, Michael (Eds.), International Relations and the European Union, New York, NY 2005, p. 376.

[18] Cf. **Janz**, Louis, Die Geschichte der europäischen Einigung nach den Zweiten Weltkrieg, p. 82.

[19] Cf. **Weidenfeld**, Werner, Europa im Umbruch: Perspektiven einer neuen Ordnung des Kontinents, in: **Weidenfeld**, Werner, **Stützle**, Walther (Ed.), Abschied von der alten Ordnung: Europas neue Sicherheit, Gütersloh 1990, p. 7.

which the concept of Europe is based[21], no guiding roadmap. The one intention that was obvious was the political unification[22]. In order to make this vision come true, institutions like the progressive implementation of an economic union, a monetary union and a common market were of utmost importance.[23]

Although the European Union and its political leaders have "not yet succeeded in crafting a common European sense of 'who we are'"[24] in defining an EU-identity for the people in the European Union member states, it is by far not too late. As stated before, the project of the European Union is a one-of-a-kind experiment; there is no existing comparable transnational structure. John F. Kennedy, a non-European, phrased it as follows: "Those who dare to fail miserably can achieve greatly." No one knows what lies ahead, but one has to dare, one has to have the courage to act and to foster movement. The development of the European Union could be regarded as moving at a snail's pace[25], but yet it is important to acknowledge that despite its pace, it is moving constantly forward.

a. What happened so far

This brief discussion of the road the European Union has taken so far will predominantly focus on main events after the end of World War II. Nonetheless it is important to note that European civil societies of the 19th century already aligned themselves to the elements of peace, the rule of law and democracy and openly spoke their mind.[26] Revolutions in many European countries, aiming at establishing a constitution, demanding the right to participate, and asking for civil rights to be legally acknowledged may illustrate this fact.

The European continent has suffered from wars and national hatred for centuries; it was far from being a singular entity in any way until the beginning of the 20th century. After World War I, a primary stage of a pacifistic European idealism grew out of the rubble.[27] "[B]ereft of

---

[20] **Wæver**, Ole, **Kelstrup**, Morten, Europe and its nations, p. 65.
[21] The five main fragments in the dominant discourses on Europe were: the role of Europe as a geographical concept, the concept of liberty, Europe as Christendom, the balance of power and European civilization, cf. ibid.
[22] Cf. **Janz**, Louis, Die Geschichte der europäischen Einigung nach den Zweiten Weltkrieg, p. 81.
[23] Cf. ibid., pp. 93 f.
[24] **Checkel**, Jeffrey T., **Katzenstein**, Peter J., The politicization of European identities, in: **Checkel**, Jeffrey T., **Katzenstein**, Peter J. (Eds.), European Identity, Cambridge 2009, p. 1.
[25] **Janz**, Louis, Die Geschichte der europäischen Einigung nach den Zweiten Weltkrieg, p. 109.
[26] Cf. **Schmale**, Wolfgang, Geschichte und Zukunft der Europäischen Identität, p. 103.
[27] Cf. **Szyszko**, Agata, Die kulturelle Identität Europas als ideen- und begriffsgeschichtliches Konzept, in: **Birk**, Eberhard (Ed.), Aspekte einer europäischen Identität, Fürstenfeldbruck 2004, p. 16.

11

a firm psychological basis"[28] and under the Nazi-occupation of Europe, the merits of the idea of Europe became ambiguous though.[29] Ravaged by war and destruction, bemoaning the loss of millions of people and economically devastated, Europe experienced its zero hour in the aftermath of World War II. The founding fathers of the European unification primarily initiated this project in order to restore peace in Europe[30] and "to eradicate unnecessary suffering from Western Europe whether caused by interstate war or by economic collapse"[31]. However, the occupying powers, namely the United States of America and the Soviet Union, were not interested in fostering an independent Europe[32] and aimed at a restoration on a nation-state level instead.[33] Given the amount of challenging tasks, the European national governments' point of interest was their own country at first, not the seminal ideas of Europe.[34] It was imperative to rebuild entire nations, including their societies, their economy, their political structure and their international relations, too. In this environment, considerable courage and dedication was needed to achieve a European unification[35], given the tremendous dimension of fragmentation and devastation.

One first step to foster closer cooperation and interaction took place in Geneva in 1947 when the United Nations Economic Commission for Europe (UNECE or ECE) was founded[36]. It was the first supraregional sub-organization of the United Nations. Just one year later, 18 European states joined the Organization for European Economic Cooperation (OEEC).[37] In the very same year, the Hague Congress took place. It was the first meeting of such a kind, presided over by former British Prime Minister Winston Churchill, in which some 800 politicians of Western European countries came together to explore future framework requirements of a unified Europe.[38] Simultaneously launched, the Marshall Plan contributed much to the European unifying process in the economic sphere – even though it should be noted that the US was in a position to impose more pressure which could have resulted in the creation of a common European political structure.[39]

---

[28] **Checkel**, Jeffrey T., **Katzenstein**, Peter J., The politicization of European identities, p. 4.
[29] Cf. **Schäfers**, Bernhard, Sozialstruktur und sozialer Wandel in Deutschland, p. 296.
[30] Cf. **Westerwelle**, Guido, Der Wert Europas, p. 91.
[31] **Linklater**, Andrew, A European Civilising Process, p. 376.
[32] Cf. **Gruner**, Wolf D., **Woyke**, Wichard, Europa-Lexikon. Länder – Politik – Institutionen, München 2004, p. 42.
[33] Cf. ibid.
[34] Cf. ibid., pp. 42 f.
[35] Cf. **Szyszko**, Agata, Die kulturelle Identität Europas als ideen- und begriffsgeschichtliches Konzept, p. 16.
[36] Cf. **Janz**, Louis, Die Geschichte der europäischen Einigung nach den Zweiten Weltkrieg, p. 83.
[37] Cf. ibid.
[38] Cf. **Hick**, Alan, Die Europäische Bewegung, in: **Loth**, Wilfried (Ed.), Die Anfänge der Europäischen Integration 1945-1950, Bonn 1990, p. 241.
[39] Cf. **Janz**, Louis, Die Geschichte der europäischen Einigung nach den Zweiten Weltkrieg, p. 84.

The next decisive step was the Schuman Declaration of May 9th 1950[40]. French Foreign Minister Robert Schuman proposed the establishment of a community working supranationally, organizing coal and steel industries in France, Germany and other European countries willing to join.[41] His forward-looking plan was implemented through the foundations of the European Coal and Steel Community (ECSC) and the Treaty of Paris.[42] In the field of military unification, the treaty of a European Defense Community (EDC), based on a proposal by René Pleven, then-French Prime Minister regarding a pan-European defense force, was signed on May 27th 1952 by the members of the ECSC[43], but the French Parliament denied its ratification. Thus, the idea of the EDC was never realized. With the Treaty of Rome (the Treaty establishing the European Economic Community), signed on May 25th 1957, the European Economic Community (EEC) and the European Atomic Energy Community (EAEC or EURATOM) were founded.[44]

The division of Germany and the iron curtain, an ideological as well as a physical boundary, led to a separation between Western and Eastern Europe in a hitherto unknown intensity.[45] The bipolarity between the Soviet-dominated Warsaw Pact on the one hand and the European Community and NATO member states on the other hand, as well as the subsequent political, economic, military and social tensions made history. The Cold War dominated the second half of the 20th century. But it also "gave way to debate in terms of Europe"[46] due to the geographical closeness and the gradually defining of the European Community's role. With the reunification of Germany in 1989 and the collapse of the Eastern Bloc, Europe witnessed "a historic turning point in [its] history"[47]. From then on, its actions were no longer reactive, but started showing constructive and forming traits[48], giving a hand to "post-socialist societies which were struggling to achieve economic prosperity and political stability"[49]. Thus, a multitude of new EU member states' incentives to join the EU was initially based upon mere economic calculations rather than on the founding ideas of the post-World War II momentum.[50] The Maastricht Treaty, signed on February 7th, 1992, legally avouched the four great free-

---

[40] This date is regarded as the *hour of birth* of the EU and is celebrated as the Europe Day since 1986, commemorating Schumans far-reaching idea and speech.
[41] Cf. **Janz**, Louis, Die Geschichte der europäischen Einigung nach den Zweiten Weltkrieg, p. 86.
[42] Cf. ibid., p. 89.
[43] Cf. ibid., pp. 89 f.
[44] Cf. ibid., p. 93.
[45] Cf. ibid., p. 80.
[46] **Wæver**, Ole, **Kelstrup**, Morten, Europe and its nations, p. 64.
[47] **Weidendfeld**, Werner, **Janning**, Josef, After 1989: The Emerge of a new Europe, in: **Weidendfeld**, Werner, **Janning**, Josef (Eds.), Global Responsibilities: Europe in Tomorrow's World, Gütersloh 1991, p. 12.
[48] Cf. **Wæver**, Ole, **Kelstrup**, Morten, Europe and its nations, p. 64.
[49] **Linklater**, Andrew, A European Civilizing Process, p. 368.
[50] Cf. **Kielmannsegg**, Peter Graf, Integration und Demokratie, in: **Jachtenfuchs**, Markus, **Kohler-Koch**, Beate (Eds.), Europäische Integration, Opladen 2003, p. 50.

doms (freedom of trade, passenger traffic, services and capital) and presented the Three Pillars of the European Union.[51] With the Lisbon Treaty, signed on December 13th, 2007, which adopted, with regard to contents, the 2005 Treaty establishing a Constitution for Europe, the EU now has a constitution-like legal framework. Even today, no proper term has been found to describe the political nature of the EU – which makes it one of a kind, "sui generis"[52].

The face of Europe has changed remarkably over the last five decades. Never has this continent seen a comparable era of peace, stability, prosperity and harmony. The number of its member states has more than quadruplicated since the foundation of the ECSC. Given its constant advancements and adjustments to internal and external requirements, the EU today is "clearly far more than a conventional international organization"[53]. Forging a common destiny[54] on various levels, the EU has developed far beyond mere economic integration traditionalists envisioned.

b. Analyzing present and potential future challenges for the EU

A united Europe is anticipated to be the best possible solution to prepare its member states for present and future challenges[55] through sustainable and stabilizing politics. For centuries, "Western Europeans have devoted a great deal of energy to killing each other"[56] instead of cooperating and showing solidarity with neighboring countries. Owing to the economical, political and social unification expedited by the EU, military conflicts among member states have become almost unimaginable.[57] The EU represents the longest period of peace and stability ever experienced on European soil. Thus, potential threats are hardly expected to come from other member states since "threat makes us choose sides"[58]. Due to historical experiences, the EU prevented various dangers of all kinds so far. Referring to neofunctionalism, endogenous preferences and spillover effects foster appropriate developments.[59]

---

[51] Cf. **Hänsch**, Klaus, Perspektiven der europäischen Integration, in: **Leiße**, Olaf (Ed.), Die Europäische Union nach dem Vertrag von Lissabon, Wiesbaden 2010, p. 70.
[52] **McCormick**, John, Understanding the European Union, p. 22.
[53] Ibid.
[54] Cf. **Weidenfeld**, Werner, **Turek**, Jürgen, Wie Zukunft entsteht, p. 178.
[55] Cf. **Westerwelle**, Guido, Der Wert Europas, p. 90.
[56] **Calhoun**, Craig, The Virtues of Inconsistency: Identity and Plurality in the Conceptualization of Europe, in: **Cederman**, Lars-Erik (Ed.), Constructing Europe's Identity. The external dimension, Boulder, CO 2001, p. 37.
[57] Cf. **Weidenfeld**, Werner, **Turek**, Jürgen, Wie Zukunft entsteht, p. 178.
[58] **Checkel**, Jeffrey T., **Katzenstein**, Peter J., Conclusion – European identity in context, in: **Checkel**, Jeffrey T., **Katzenstein**, Peter J. (Eds.), European Identity, Cambridge 2009, p. 214.
[59] Cf. **Schimmelpfennig**, Frank, Zwischen Neo- und Postfunktionalismus: Die Integrationstheorien und die Eurokrise, in: Politische Vierteljahreszeitschrift, 2012 (3), p. 395.

In order to analyze present and potential future challenges for the EU, one has to classify them first. So there will be a selection of (1) internal EU-issues, (2) threats coming from other countries and (3) ecological factors.

First and foremost, the cleavage between the EU-citizens and the proceeding European conciliation does not stop increasing.[60] Due to the continuous lack of legitimacy and democracy[61], the EU-citizens feel neither represented nor personally addressed. Therefore, many of them have developed an indifferent attitude towards European polity.[62] Decisions made in Brussels, regarding more and more aspects of everyday life, are often perceived as burdens.[63] Particularly when it comes to mere cost-benefit calculations[64], donor EU member states weight their own contributions against what they might receive or be given back by member states that are supported. As there is no stable nor acknowledged EU-identity, transnational solidarity is remarkably low.[65] Since 2008, when the economic crisis started spreading globally, the EU had to learn what solidarity among member states really means. National debt crises of Greece, Spain, Portugal, Cyprus and Italy burdened and even exhausted the intra-European relations sustainably and there is still no end in sight.[66] The economic strength and success of the EU has been the most appealing argument in the course of the European unification[67] but being equitable partners collaborating in an economic system[68] makes demands on both sides. Given the distinctly diverse levels of economic power, some states claimed economic aid[69] in order to be given a chance to catch up with the *economic locomotives* of the EU. Due to traditional rivalries and stereotypes[70], friction among member states will likely prove a roadblock to success, and will have to be dealt with in the future.

Another component of the crucial test the EU is currently facing, as well as the issue it will have to confront in the future, is the multitude of cultures that exist within Europe. In some cases, the reach of a culture does not even match the geographical borders[71]. Indeed, thinking

---

[60] Cf. **Hänsch**, Klaus, Perspektiven der europäischen Integration, p. 69.

[61] Cf. **Kielmannsegg**, Peter Graf, Integration und Demokratie, p. 53.

[62] Cf. **Meyer**, Thomas, Die Identität Europas, Frankfurt/Main 2004, p. 10.

[63] Cf. **Kielmannsegg**, Peter Graf, Integration und Demokratie, p. 51.

[64] Cf. **Göler**, Daniel, Die Grenzen des "Cost-of-Non-Europe"-Narrativs: Anmerkungen zur Sinnstiftung der Europäischen Integration, in: integration, 2012 (2), p. 132.

[65] Cf. **Schimmelpfennig**, Frank, Zwischen Neo- und Postfunktionalismus, p. 396.

[66] Cf. **Schimmelpfennig**, Frank, Zwischen Neo- und Postfunktionalismus, p. 394.

[67] Cf. **Seidl-Hohenveldern**, Ignaz, Fragen zu Großeuropa, in: **Seidl-Hohenveldern**, Ignaz (Eds.), Auf dem Weg nach Europa – Fragen zur europäischen Integration, Köln 1991, p. 6.

[68] Cf. **Berting**, Jan, **Braak**, Hans van de, L'identité culturelle de la »Grande Europe« : mythe ou réalité, in : **Viallain-Gandossi**, Christiane, **Bochmann**, Klaus, **Metzeltin**, Michel, **Schäffner**, Christina (Eds.), Le concept de l'Europe dans le processus de la CSCE, Tübingen 1990, p. 35.

[69] Cf. **Seidl-Hohenveldern**, Ignaz, Fragen zu Großeuropa, p. 6.

[70] Cf. **McCormick**, John, Understanding the European Union, p. 32.

[71] Cf. **Berting**, Jan, **Braak**, Hans van de, L'identité culturelle de la »Grande Europe«, p. 35.

within the limits of nations restrains European integration. Nationalism must be countered to allow Europe to become "a place where institutional arrangements foster a plurality of identities"[72]. In the same vein, the EU also has to foster a sustainable integration of Central European countries that are "no longer allies of the USSR, nor are they members of NATO, nor are they formally neutral, nor are they organized regionally in security terms"[73]. Finding a satisfying and wise solution in this domain is imperative and demands a constructive and positive dialogue among all member states.

Furthermore, the EU shoulders great responsibilities. Due to its economic and political influence, it is dealing with "new and global responsibilities"[74], e.g. humanitarian aid and development assistance and even beyond EU-borders, when it comes to foreign and security policy[75].

Referring to the second sort of challenges – threats coming from other countries – the question of migration[76] will undoubtedly be one of the most urgent ones. It is "a major political question and […] the subject of turbulent debates in the public sphere"[77] where "major political actors [agree on] a more restrictive, control-oriented approach."[78] With plenty of immigrants, may they be "prompted by conflict, the fear of repression or just sheer lack of hope."[79], Ultimately, it should be said, Western European countries fear a further crisis of their national identities.[80]

Apart from migration, the rise of newly industrializing countries and an immense growth of population – China, India and Brazil[81] – create profound changes in the economic and political world order.[82] The EU has to define and to defend its position in order to remain meaning-

---

[72] **Calhoun**, Craig, The Virtues of Inconsistency, p. 53.
[73] **Heisbourg**, François, Restructuring European Security, in: **Weidendfeld**, Werner, **Janning**, Josef (Eds.), Global Responsibilities: Europe in Tomorrow's World, Gütersloh 1991, p. 101.
[74] **Weidendfeld**, Werner, **Janning**, Josef, After 1989: The Emerge of a new Europe, p. 12.
[75] Cf. **Westerwelle**, Guido, Der Wert Europas, p. 91.
[76] "In the context of the EU, cultural readings of migration emerge in relation to three themes. The first is the cultural (and possibly racial) significance of border controls and limitations of free movement. The second is the question of integration or assimilation of migrants into the domestic societies of the member states. The third is the relationship between European integration and the development of multicultural societies" in: **Huysmans**, Jef, European Identity and Migration Policies, in: **Cederman**, Lars-Erik (Ed.), Constructing Europe's Identity. The external dimension, Boulder, CO 2001, p. 198.
[77] Ibid., p. 189.
[78] Ibid.
[79] **Heisbourg**, François, Restructuring European Security, p. 98.
[80] Cf. **Mitchell**, Mark, **Russell**, Dave, Immigration, citizenship and the nation-state in the new Europe, in: **Jenkins**, Brian, **Spyros**, A. Sofos (Eds.), Nation and Identity in Contemporary Europe, London 1996, p. 73.
[81] Cf. **Hänsch**, Klaus, Perspektiven der europäischen Integration, p. 75.
[82] Cf. **Westerwelle**, Guido, Der Wert Europas, p. 90.

ful. Acting individually, no European nation would truly be in a position to negotiate with global enterprises or global powers.[83]

Finally, one must return to the matter of responsibilities. Although environmental effects do not affect only specific countries but are experienced globally, its political strength and its state of the art of science and technology oblige the EU to take measures for the protection of the environment[84] and the handling of climate change.[85] In order to preserve the world for future generations, the EU has to set an example and implement international standards through its environmental policy.

Recapitulatory, the amount of challenges for the EU in various areas are manifold. But the EU has proven itself flexible and adaptive so far, since its entire history can be seen as a learning process.[86] Europe has never been an exclusively European topic[87] nor will it ever be due to its global interconnectedness on all levels. The EU's uncontested strength in facing these challenges is rooted in its inner plurality.[88]

c. Together we stand, divided we fall: Expounding the necessity of a mutually acknowledged EU-identity

Taking into consideration the supremely favorable development of the EU and its powerful position in the world today, why would there be a need for a mutually acknowledged identity? There has not been an EU-identity so far and still the Union stands tall. But as in everyday life, the true stability of relations is revealed in times of crises. Given the ongoing financial crisis and the challenges that are in the offing, the lack of an EU-identity, shared by the EU-citizens, is precarious. EU-internal debates are no longer exercised on a professional and rational level, but emotional and biased towards old antagonisms.

As mentioned before, the European continent has never witnessed a similarly long phase of peace so far: Since 1945, there has been no armed conflict amongst the member states of the EU.[89] Due to legal, political and economic interdependencies[90], the EU succeeded in pacifying a multitude of former belligerent countries. Howbeit "nation-states have become since the

---

[83] Cf. **Hänsch**, Klaus, Perspektiven der europäischen Integration, p. 75.
[84] Cf. **Berting**, Jan, **Braak**, Hans van de, L'identité culturelle de la "Grande Europe", p. 43.
[85] Cf. **Hänsch**, Klaus, Perspektiven der europäischen Integration, p. 69.
[86] Cf. **Kohlhase**, Norbert, Strategien der Europapolitik, in: **Weidenfeld**, Werner (Eds.), Die Identität Europas, München 1985, p. 263.
[87] Cf. **Muschg**, Adolf, Was ist europäisch ?, Bonn 2005, p. 15.
[88] Cf. **Szyszko**, Agata, Die kulturelle Identität Europas als ideen- und begriffsgeschichtliches Konzept, p. 22.
[89] Cf. **Enzensberger**, Hans Magnus, Sanftes Monster Brüssel oder die Entmündigung Europas, Berlin 2011, p. 7.
[90] Cf. **Kohlhase**, Norbert, Strategien der Europapolitik, p. 257.

last century the natural political form"[91], the EU member states are endowed with a shared inheritance.[92] Never before was the continent likewise thrice blessed with wealth, rights, and perspectives[93] like these days. In order to enshrine these achievements, the EU has to "search for an essence"[94]. It must define its illusions, goals, and objectives so as to create a normative identity.[95]

With integration being the exclusive alternative[96], the EU has to recollect its supranational[97] identity markers and envisage a reflection "in public debate"[98] Only by starting from the citizen's level, self-determination on a global level[99] can be successful. A legitimate and democratic imprint is indispensable if a political identity[100] is supposed to emphasize membership and the willingness to participate.

Consequently, the EU has to foster the genesis of an EU-identity that is mutually acknowledged to override internal friction, to rekindle European solidarity again, and to define its position in the world in the future. Europe, more specifically the EU, can only survive united. To visualize the situation, one can imagine the individual countries of the EU as young trees. If a tress is located alone, there is no protection from any side. Wind, rain, snow, and further kinds of weather harry it without hindrance. It is solely in a group of trees – a copse or a forest – where stronger and more resistant trees give shelter to smaller ones and render their growth possible. They are rooted in the same earth and are bathed in the same sunlight. Yet every tree is an individual and always will be.

d. The EU White Paper on Sport

The Treaty of Rome did not mention sport in any way[101]. This neglectful treatment on the level of governance lasted until 1985, the Milan European Summit. The EC Council of Minis-

---

[91] **Jacobs**, Dirk, **Maier**, Robert, European Identity: construct, fact, fiction, in: **Gastelaars**, Marja, **Ruijter**, Arie de (Eds.), A United Europe. The Quest for a Multifaceted Identity, Maastricht 1998, p. 17.

[92] Cf. **Berting**, Jan, **Braak**, Hans van de, L'identité culturelle de la "Grande Europe", p. 45.

[93] Cf. **Cohn-Bendit**, Daniel, **Verhofstadt**, Guy, Für Europa! Ein Manifest, Antwerpen 2012, p. 11.

[94] **Bifulco**, Marco, In search of an identity for Europe, Bonn 1998, p. 3.

[95] Cf. **Schmale**, Wolfgang, Geschichte und Zukunft der Europäischen Identität, p. 131.

[96] Cf. **Hollaschke**, Gerhard, Die EG-Integration zwischen Anpassung und Veränderung. Demokratietheoretische Überlegungen und institutionelle Reformen, in: **Strübel**, Michael (Ed.), Wohin treibt Europa? Der EG-Binnenmarkt und das Gemeinsame Europäische Haus, Marburg 1990, p. 56.

[97] Cf. **Szyszko**, Agata, Die kulturelle Identität Europas als ideen- und begriffsgeschichtliches Konzept, p. 22.

[98] Cf. **Checkel**, Jeffrey T., **Katzenstein**, Peter J., The politicization of European identities, p. 4.

[99] Cf. **Szyszko**, Agata, Die kulturelle Identität Europas als ideen- und begriffsgeschichtliches Konzept, p. 11.

[100] Cf. **Meyer**, Thomas, Die Identität Europas, p. 21.

[101] Cf. **Tokarski**, Walter, Europa in Bewegung – Der Sport im „Europa der Bürger" gewinnt Konturen, in: **Tokarski**, Walter, **Petry**, Karen, **Schulz**, Norbert (Eds.), Brennpunkte der Sportwissenschaft. Sport im „Europa

ters decided to use sport as an instrument for communication and public relations.[102] Thus, the Adonnino Report highlighted the fact that sport is a preeminent medium to tighten the EC-citizens' sense of belonging to the European Community.[103] With the foundation of the European Sports Forum in 1991[104] the European Commission acted on the suggestion of the European Olympic Committee (EOC).[105] In this vein, various sports associations of EU member states were given the chance to communicate. Until the Treaty of Lisbon, the role of sports has been increasingly carved out in various documents and treaties.[106] With the Treaty of Lisbon sport has been legally pinned individually in an EU-treaty for the first time.[107] Thus, the EU can refer to a legal basis in order to support member states on the domain of sport[108] since a defined EU competence has been introduced. Due to the enhanced competences, the Directorate-General Education and Culture of the European Commission[109] (DG EAC) is being regarded more highly.[110]

Within the EU, questions on sports are dealt within DG EAC; moreover the European Parliament runs a Committee responsible for education, culture, youth, *sport and the cultural and educational aspects of the EU's* media policy.[111]

The EU White Paper on Sport is the first document on the level of the EU formulating clear objectives.[112] Containing recommendations for future European policies and propounding strategies how sports can be embedded in various political domains, it was presented on July 11th, 2007 by the European Commission.[113] Despite the small volume of only 21 pages, its

---

der Bürger". Neue Beiträge zum Zusammenwachsen des Sports im Europäischen Binnenmarkt, 1994 (1), p. 5.

[102] Cf. **Danckert**, Peter, Kraftmaschine Parlament. Der Sportausschuss und die Sportpolitik des Bundes, Aachen 2009, p. 230.

[103] Cf. **Kepper**, Christophe de, Die Europäische Union und der Sport, in: **Schimke**, Martin (Ed.), Sport in der Europäischen Union, Heidelberg 1996, p. 4.

[104] Cf. **Kepper**, Christophe de, Die Europäische Union und der Sport, p. 5.

[105] Cf. **Tokarski**, Walter, **Steinbach**, Dirk, Spuren. Sportpolitik und Sportstrukturen in der Europäischen Union, p. 56.

[106] E.g. The EU member states agreed on paying more regard to sports in the Amsterdam Treaty. In the Treaty of Nice, they stressed the social and cultural values of sport. Neither of the treaties was legally binding though, cf. http://europa.eu/legislation_summaries/institutional_affairs/treaties/amsterdam_treaty/index_en.htm and http://eur-lex.europa.eu/en/treaties/dat/12001C/pdf/12001C_EN.pdf

[107] **Singer**, Otto, Sportpolitik der Europäischen Union nach dem Lissabon-Vertrag, http://www.bundestag.de/dokumente/analysen/2010/Sportpolitik_EU.pdf, p. 3.

[108] Ibid., p. 11.

[109] Cf. http://ec.europa.eu/dgs/education_culture/

[110] **Singer**, Otto, Sportpolitik der Europäischen Union nach dem Lissabon-Vertrag, p. 13.

[111] Cf. **Tokarski**, Walter, **Steinbach**, Dirk, Spuren. Sportpolitik und Sportstrukturen in der Europäischen Union, p. 56.

[112] Cf. **Danckert**, Peter, Kraftmaschine Parlament, p. 238.

[113] Cf. ibid., p. 237.

tripartite[114] structure is strategically clear and it extensively[115] analyses all possible spheres of sports.[116] The White Paper on Sport comes with three accompanying documents: The action plan *Pierre de Coubertin[117]*, the Commission Staff Working Document *Background and Context* and the Commission Staff Working Document *Impact Assessment.*[118] Hence, the White Paper on Sport can be seen as a guideline for sport-related projects in the coming years. Despite the cross-border effects and the internationality of sport[119], this document "shows a European Commission that is aware of its limitations to intervene in the sports sector"[120] since it has to respect national sports associations' sovereignty. Owing to the interdependencies of professional sport and the economic sector, the sector of popular sports is hardly ever mentioned. The emphasis of the White Paper is clearly on professional sport, based on the well-known potentials of sport in general.

In summary, the White Paper on Sport can be regarded as the most comprehensive and visionary document on sport produced so far by the EU. It reveals that many problems of sports (e.g. doping, gambling, etc.) can be solved on the level of the EU only.[121] Despite the "relatively new"[122] interest in sport governance, the extent and the impact of upcoming actions based on this document can be expected to be profound.

---

[114] The societal role of sport, the economic dimension of sport and the organization of sport, cf. **Europäische Kommission**, Mitteilung zum Sport (2011). Entwicklung der europäischen Dimension des Sports, Brüssel 2011, p. 3 f.

[115] Cf. **Danckert**, Peter, Kraftmaschine Parlament, p. 238.

[116] The White Paper on Sport appreciates the societal role of sports, defines the role of sport in education and training, fosters the promotion of volunteering, takes side effects like integration and the fight against racism into consideration, explores the economic dimension of sport, acknowledges the organization of sport - primarily professional sports and drafts follow-up measures.

[117] In this document, the measures mentioned in the White Paper on Sport are embodied. The action plan contains 53 concrete sport-related suggestions that intend to guide the European Commission's sport policy in the upcoming years.

[118] Cf. **Danckert**, Peter, Kraftmaschine Parlament, p. 237.

[119] Cf. **Hansen**, Hans, Europa wächst zusammen, in: **Rydzy-Götz**, Marlis (Ed.), Die Europäische Gemeinschaft und der Sport, Frankfurt a.M. 1992, p. 3.

[120] **García**, Borja, The Governance of European Sport, in: **Dine**, Philip, **Crosson**, Seán (Eds.), Sport, Representation and Evolving Identities in Europe, Oxford 2010, p. 47.

[121] Cf. **Danckert**, Peter, Kraftmaschine Parlament, p. 240.

[122] **García**, Borja, The Governance of European Sport, p. 29.

2. The European Union and its prospective identity

a. One multifaceted EU-identity

Referring to the prevailing view, it can be said that there is "no stable core, no given European identity"[123] which would be perceived by Europeans.[124] In order to specify the term of identity in this study, one has to draw a line between a European identity in general and the EU-identity in particular. To what extent are these two identities synonymous[125]? What aspects cause a differentiation? Bruter[126] points out that the definition of the terms of perception of *Europe* is decisive. He contrasts a cultural point of view from a political one.[127] This information enables politicians to develop specifically tailored governance projects in order to foster the genesis of an EU-identity. The EU is predominantly experienced as a "political, value and economic community"[128] and as a "political entity based on universal values"[129]. This knowledge challenges politicians in finding an appropriate answer to the question of what kind of EU-identity should be generated[130] – what are its basic contents?

This second section aims at developing a solid blueprint of a potential EU-identity, taking into consideration that the EU is a political system *sui generis*[131] and so will be its identity, viz. one cannot simply copy some national identity. Apart from that, the hereby developed EU-identity does not aim as replacing traditional national identities of EU member states.[132]

With the extensive use of the term identity in everyday language, its scientific expression has become rather diffuse and polysemous.[133] Identity is not predetermined possession, but it means the social process[134] of self-definition of individuals or groups, based on a mutually accepted embodiment of values[135]. Moreover, it is defined by inclusionary and exclusionary schemes.[136] Yet another distinction has to be made "between the subjects and the objects of

---

[123] **Wæver**, Ole, **Kelstrup**, Morten, Europe and its nations: political and cultural identities, p. 65.
[124] Cf. **Kielmannsegg**, Peter Graf, Integration und Demokratie, p. 57.
[125] Cf. **Risse**, Thomas, A Community of Europeans?, p. 50.
[126] Cf. **Bruter**, Michael, Citizens of Europe?
[127] 'Culture' in this understanding encompasses history, ethnicity, civilization, heritage, and other social similarities. 'Political identity' instead is more circumscribed and refers to the identification of citizens with particular political institutions such as the EU, cf. **Risse**, Thomas, A Community of Europeans?, p. 50.
[128] Ibid.
[129] Ibid., p. 51.
[130] Cf. **Datler**, Georg, Europäische Identität jenseits der Demos-Fiktion, p. 59.
[131] Cf. **Hix**, Simon, The Study of the European Community, p. 324.
[132] Cf. **Wagner**, Hartmut, Bezugspunkte europäischer Identität, p. 13.
[133] **Stelter**, Reinhard, Du bist wie dein Sport, p. 19.
[134] Cf. **Meyer**, Thomas, Die Identität Europas, p. 24.
[135] Cf. **Czarny**, Raphaël, Existe-t-il une identité européenne ?
[136] Cf. **Schmale**, Wolfgang, Geschichte und Zukunft der Europäischen Identität, p. 37.

identification, in other words, who – for example, elites or ordinary citizens – identifies with whom or what – for example, gender, nation, or Europe"[137]. So, "identities emerge in the very process by which individuals and social groups make sense of who they are and what they want"[138]. However, every definition has to be seen as a part[139] of one of diverse[140] individual theoretical approaches that should be regarded as a whole.

Although the question of political identity is not new[141], "the jargon is newly fashionable"[142] and it is of interest to many political theorists. Due to its uniqueness, the lack of analogs of supranational structures like the EU[143] challenges theorists of all disciplines[144] researching collective identities. Consequently, the "politics of European identity [are explored] by adopting a multi-disciplinary perspective"[145] in order to give consideration to the complexity of EU-identity. The responsibility of policy-makers is humongous: In "our post-modern world, we more and more exhibit multiple identities that exist in fractured and non-contiguous forms"[146]. Thence, a prospective EU-identity has to be solid, it has to be in accordance with the EU member states' desires, and it has to be mutually acknowledged to be accepted.

i. The nature of an EU-identity

With the EU's increasing profile "as a regional and international actor […] the scholarly literature on European integration has grown exponentially"[147] based on the multitude of ideas related to Europe.[148] However, the perspective has been altered: "Traditionally, empirical political scientists have been more interested in the degree to which European citizens support European integration than in the extent to which they identify with the new political entity created"[149]. So, studying the nature and the contents of an EU-identity is relatively new.[150]

---

[137] **Risse**, Thomas, A Community of Europeans?, p. 19.
[138] Ibid., p. 20.
[139] Cf. **Stelter**, Reinhard, Du bist wie dein Sport, p. 21.
[140] Cf. **Villain-Gandossi**, Christiane, **Berting**, Jan, L'Europe, loin de la fin de l'histoire, p. 543.
[141] "The history of the European idea shows that it has appeared in various periods of history in a relatively clear form, then disappeared for long stretches, then reappeared with partly new meanings and with twists and turns giving it yet new content", **Wæver**, Ole, **Kelstrup**, Morten, Europe and its nations: political and cultural identities, p. 65.
[142] **Calhoun**, Craig, The Virtues of Inconsistency: Identity and Plurality in the Conceptualization of Europe, p. 38.
[143] Cf. **Wagner**, Hartmut, Bezugspunkte europäischer Identität, p. 14.
[144] Cf. **Fligstein**, Neil, Who are the Europeans and how does this matter for politics?, p. 134.
[145] **Checkel**, Jeffrey T., **Katzenstein**, Peter J., The politicization of European identities, p. 2.
[146] **Mitchell**, Mark, **Russell**, Dave, Immigration, citizenship and the nation-state in the new Europe, p. 76.
[147] **Dominguez**, Roberto, **Royo**, Sebastián, The Study of the European Integration Process in the United States, in: European Political Science, 2012 (3), p. 305.
[148] Cf. **Wæver**, Ole, **Kelstrup**, Morten, Europe and its nations: political and cultural identities, p. 65.
[149] **Bruter**, Michael, Citizens of Europe?, p. 3.

The range of disciplines[151] investigating the matter of identity has also increased enormously, being an interdisciplinary seduction[152] nowadays.

Referring to the EU as a project, Habermas predicted a failure if "it is attempted in the format of the nineteenth-century nation state"[153]. With every member state being an independent and individual nation state, an EU claiming the same political format, thus incapacitating its members, would be defeating itself.

Risse differentiates between inclusive and exclusive nationalists arguing that this kind of perception outweighs the presumed distinction between Europeans and nationalists.[154] Coevally, he assumes the existence of a basic consciousness of being an EU-citizen.

Wæver's discourse analysis approaches the matter how a prospective EU-identity is configured and investigates different mechanisms. He emphasizes that "most of the existing work on this issue connects identity to the question of legitimacy"[155], i.e. with the EU being a political structure sui generis, does its identity require the same legitimating features as traditional political identities?

Wagner tested to test identity markers for three functional criteria: delimitation, perception, and plausibility.[156] The term of delimitation is to be found frequently in pertinent literature, aiming at expounding the theory of constructing "some external 'Other'"[157] by contrast to the EU-identity. It is hence a supportive and favorable method to increase the popularity of this transnational kind of identity by defining what is not European.[158]

Kielsmannsegg stated that collective identities emanate from communities of communication, experience and memory. In view of Europe, however, he concludes that Europe does not rely on communication, it is hardly endued with memories, and it possesses only few common memories.[159] Thus, Europe can be seen "as an imagined community"[160]. His concept will be

---

[150] This topic started gaining recognition after the Cold War only, when the hitherto self-definition of the EU came to an end, cf. **Wagner**, Hartmut, Bezugspunkte europäischer Identität, p. 14.
[151] The notion of identity has been studied mainly by philosophers and psychologists before attracting the attention of historians, sociologists or political scientists, too, cf. **Bruter**, Michael, Citizens of Europe?, p. 8.
[152] Cf. **Meyer**, Thomas, Die Identität Europas, p. 7.
[153] **Wæver**, Ole, **Kelstrup**, Morten, Europe and its nations: political and cultural identities, p. 67.
[154] Inclusive nationalists identify with their nation state and the EU whilst exclusive nationalists hold exclusive national identities, cf. **Risse**, Thomas, A Community of Europeans?, p. 43.
[155] **Wæver**, Ole, Discursive Approaches, in: **Wiener**, Antje, **Diez** Thomas (Eds.), European Integration Theory, Oxford 2009, pp. 174 f.
[156] Cf. **Wagner**, Hartmut, Bezugspunkte europäischer Identität, p. 93.
[157] **Wæver**, Ole, Discursive Approaches, p. 175.
[158] e.g. by a "negative casting of Japan, Turkey, and/or Islam, Russia or maybe increasingly the US", **Wæver**, Ole, Discursive Approaches, p. 175.
[159] Cf. **Kielmannsegg**, Peter Graf, Integration und Demokratie, p. 58.
[160] **Risse**, Thomas, A Community of Europeans?, p. 43.

used in the following to evaluate the significance and the verisimilitude of each of the seven components presented.

As obvious as it might be that only a mutually acknowledged EU-identity can sustainably stabilize in the long run the EU, the fact that it is actually possible and the question whether it might be desirable "is subject to profound controversy"[161]. Its possibility can be derived from already existing components which will be expounded in the following chapters. Thus, it will be shown, that an EU-identity will not be created ex-nihilo, but that these basics are available and have to be noticed.[162] The European Union has been intended to be a peaceful, democratic project[163] and so should be the process forging its identity.

Its major characteristic is its process-related, dynamic[164] nature. Since "identities flow through multiple networks and create new patterns of identification"[165], this project has to be constantly organized to keep this social process running. Thus, its identity will become a source of democratic vitality for the EU.[166] The most important processes of the past centuries[167] have their seeds in Europe and then spread out to conquer the world. Since one might demur that the dynamism could be a threat to the EU's stability[168], it has to be said that an ever-changing world cannot be stopped, nor has any kind of identity been encapsulated from internal or external influences. As a logical consequence, a sustainable EU-identity has to be grounded on basic and solid components, yet it has to be flexible enough to adapt to necessary modernizations.

Secondly, politicity is a further trait of a prospective EU-identity. As aforementioned, the view on Europe can be defined as either political or cultural. In the case of the EU, the "belonging to politically relevant human groups and political structures"[169] clearly places the emphasis on the political component – without suspending the cultural concept[170] completely.

---

[161] **Bohne**, Eberhard, EU and US Security Strategies from the Perspective of National and European Identities, Speyer 2006, p. 13.
[162] Cf. **Toussaint**, Thomas, Identité européenne: la face cachée de la crise, http://www.lemonde.fr/idees/article/2012/07/18/identite-europeenne-la-face-cachee-de-la-crise_1734603_3232.html, [online] 05.01.2013.
[163] Cf. **Jacobs**, Dirk, **Maier**, Robert, European Identity: construct, fact, fiction, p. 20.
[164] Cf. **Góra**, Magdalena, **Mach**, Zdzisław, Democracy and Identity in Europe after Enlargment, in: **Góra**, Magdalena, **Mach**, Zdzisław, **Zielińska**, Katarzyna (Eds), Collective Identity and Democracy in the Enlarging Europe, Frankfurt a.M. 2012, p. 13.
[165] **Checkel**, Jeffrey T., **Katzenstein**, Peter J., Conclusion – European identity in context, p. 213.
[166] Cf. **Meyer**, Thomas, Die Identität Europas, p. 233.
[167] Especially achievements like the Enlightenment and its philosophical and political consequences, the rule of law, the human rights, political democracy and many more were rooted in Europe, cf. **Cohn-Bendit**, Daniel, **Verhofstadt**, Guy, Für Europa!, p. 34.
[168] Cf. **Guisan**, Catherine, A political theory of identity in European integration. Memory and policies, London 2012, p. 19.
[169] **Bruter**, Michael, Citizens of Europe?, p. 1.
[170] Cf. **Wæver**, Ole, **Kelstrup**, Morten, Europe and its nations, p. 61.

A prospective is a combination of both, but with the main focus on the political part. Furthermore, the development of the EU "from a primarily economic agreement to a deeply and quintessentially political construction"[171] has shifted the reference object to another level in the course of time – yet assuming "internal cultural similarity"[172]. Especially the laical policy within the EU and the principle of tolerance amongst religions and ideologies[173] supports the politicity of the EU-identity. By excluding sensitive spheres like religion, a modern concept is more likely to be acknowledged.[174] However, when it comes to the question of nation states, the designers of the EU-identity are challenged. As it is in the name, an EU-identity has to embody the manifoldness of its member states so it can be transnationally accepted. This implies a certain degree of "selfsameness"[175] – which is a characteristic of identity.

A third trait of an EU-identity is – of course – the narrow focus on the EU and its member states. As a political system *sui generis*[176], the category of identity cannot be clearly defined; so it is neither national, not supranational in general, but one of a kind. Its internal variety is its identity's nature.[177] The Lisbon Treaty obliges the EU to "respect the equality of Member States before the Treaties as well as their national identities"[178] since this identity addresses EU-citizens of different nations. The EU as a political system has already led to a change in the perception by the rest of the world seeing "Europeans less as citizens of separate states and more as citizens of the same economic bloc"[179]. So, the EU is perceived as a "regional subsystem within the system of modern interstate relations"[180] by others. This attribution of the label EU by external actors significantly revaluates[181] the idea of an EU-identity and is essential. Thereby one of the essential premises of identity construction is fulfilled: a distinction between the EU as *self* and the rest of the world as the *other*.

---

[171] **Bruter**, Michael, Citizens of Europe?, pp. 3 f.
[172] **Calhoun**, Craig, The Virtues of Inconsistency, p. 35.
[173] Cf. **Meyer**, Thomas, Die Identität Europas, pp. 228 f.
[174] Yet it has to be said that – especially exclusive nationalists – tend to use "religion in general and Christianity in particular as the demarcation lines of Europe's in-group, **Risse**, Thomas, A Community of Europeans?, p. 53.
[175] **Calhoun**, Craig, The Virtues of Inconsistency, p. 36.
[176] Cf. ibid., p. 51.
[177] Cf. **Lichtenstein**, Dennis, Auf der Suche nach Europa: Identitätskonstruktionen und das integrative Potential von Identitätskrisen, in: **bpb magazin**, 01.03.2012, p. 6.
[178] Treaty of Lisbon, Article 3a.
[179] **McCormick**, John, Understanding the European Union. A Concise Introduction, New York, NY 2011, p. 47.
[180] **Parkhalina**, Tatyana, Europe. The concept of a »common European home«, in : **Viallain-Gandossi**, Christiane, **Bochmann**, Klaus, **Metzeltin**, Michel, **Schäffner**, Christina (Eds.), Le concept de l'Europe dans le processus de la CSCE, Tübingen 1990, p. 187.
[181] Cf. **Schmitt-Egner**, Peter, Europäische Identität. Ein konzeptioneller Leitfaden zu ihrer Erforschung und Nutzung, Baden-Baden 2012, p. 167.

Moreover, EU-identity is a collective, a social[182] identity. Collective identities are generated if social groups of at least two individuals refer to the same object[183]. They are generated through coincidence of common and individual welfare[184] and being constructed[185] through public communication. Thus, they are one level above individual identity and demand interaction with other individuals. Due to profound changes within the EU[186] during the past decades – new orientation, enlargement, and integration – existing collective identities had to adapt and were modified in order to meet the new requirements. In addition, social movement within the territory of the EU encourages the development of comprehensive collective identities[187], especially amongst young EU-citizens[188]. Given the multitude of existing identities, one can state that "cosmopolitan Europe is characterized by a positive sum relationship between nested identities"[189]. A potential EU-identity has to be embedded by its recipients into the existing cluster of identities. In order to be accepted, it has to be designed in an attractive way, interoperable enough to match with existing identities already held.

Finally, the genesis of an EU-identity demands a high degree of commitment and acceptance by the citizens. It has to be salient and persuasive enough[190] to address every single one, regardless of one's social background or one's education.[191] Modern individuals do not only refer to their roots any more, but tend to define themselves through their distinctively chosen "routes"[192]. This supports the processual trait of the EU-identity, since a person's path of life can impossibly be predicted and requires constant advancements and adaptations.

In the hereinafter seven chapters, the components of an EU-identity will be explored, taking into consideration its afore analyzed nature. These components will rely on existing attributes and show the politicity and the process-related, dynamic trait. Moreover, its explicit EU-

---

[182] Cf. **Bruter**, Michael, Citizens of Europe?, p. 9.
[183] Starting from the smallest unit, this implies couples, families, groups, rising in number to organizations, ethnies or nations, cf. **Wagner**, Hartmut, Bezugspunkte europäischer Identität, p. 17.
[184] Cf. **Schmitt-Egner**, Peter, Europäische Identität, p. 62.
[185] Cf. **Lichtenstein**, Dennis, Auf der Suche nach Europa, p. 5.
[186] Cf. **Góra**, Magdalena, **Mach**, Zdzisław, Democracy and Identity in Europe after Enlargment, p. 13.
[187] Cf. **Szyszko**, Agata, Die kulturelle Identität Europas als ideen- und begriffsgeschichtliches Konzept, p. 11.
[188] E.g. Students were given the chance to experience EU freedoms of all kinds through student exchange programs like ERASMUS, cf. **Wilke**, Kurt, „Sportstudenten auf Achse in Europa" – Europäischer Studentenaustausch, in: **Tokarski**, Walter, **Petry**, Karen, **Schulz**, Norbert (Eds.), Brennpunkte der Sportwissenschaft. Sport im „Europa der Bürger". Neue Beiträge zum Zusammenwachsen des Sports im Europäischen Binnenmarkt, 1994 (1), p. 12.
[189] **Góra**, Magdalena, **Mach**, Zdzisław, Democracy and Identity in Europe after Enlargment, p. 16.
[190] Cf. **Hapke**, Yvonne, Identity and Integration in Europe. Personal Security and the Ties of Migrants and Majority Populations to their country, München 2009, p. 91.
[191] Cf. **Körber**, Kurt A., Bergedorfer Gesprächskreis. Europa neu begründen. Kulturelle Dimensionen im Integrations- und Erweiterungsprozess, Hamburg 2003, p. 91.
[192] Cf. ibid., p. 75.

ascription will be demonstrated. Since it targets millions of EU-citizens, its collective nature is beyond controversy.

1. Territory: Border lines and exclusion

The most obvious and distinct joint possession of a group is doubtlessly the territory – with regard to the roundly accepted name, [193] the EU can rely on this fact, too. Due to its perceived implicitness, territory is predestined to be an identity marker.[194] Despite the diversity of borders[195] within the EU, the progressive transnational dislimitation of the EU[196] can be taken as a key experience for EU-citizens fostering the genesis of an EU-identity, e.g. the 1992 Maastricht Treaty grants EU-citizens the right to free movement[197] and borderless travel within "Schengenland" [198].

Critics object that the degree of abstraction of an EU-identity is a lot higher as it is for national identities.[199] The EU's political borders cannot be synchronized with its geographic borders,[200] so the territory in which the EU-identity is supposed to be effective cannot be clearly defined. The entire European continent has always been more than just a geographic area;[201] traditionally, it has served as more of a manifestation of political agendas.[202] Whilst there are natural borders in three geographic directions, there are no such limitations in the East.[203] Thence, this task has become a political issue. Moreover, it has not become obvious yet,[204] where the EU's final external borders will be located[205] since they are modified with every enlargement. Consequently there will be no solid territorial object of reference for an EU-identity as long as there is no final idea of the EU as a political structure itself. Protectionism, economically, medially and politically excluding non-EU nations, is said to secure "the identity of the national communities rather than that of the EU as a whole"[206], although these developments have "curtailed considerably the options that are available for national govern-

---

[193] Cf. **Wagner**, Hartmut, Bezugspunkte europäischer Identität, p. 53.
[194] Cf. ibid., p. 57.
[195] There are geographical, cultural, historical, economic and political borders. None of them are coinciding, cf. **Hänsch**, Klaus, Perspektiven der europäischen Integration, p. 72.
[196] Cf. **Weidenfeld**, Werner, **Turek**, Jürgen, Wie Zukunft entsteht, p. 47.
[197] Cf. **Guisan**, Catherine, A political theory of identity in European integration, p. 142.
[198] **Risse**, Thomas, A Community of Europeans?, p. 56.
[199] Cf. **Wagner**, Hartmut, Bezugspunkte europäischer Identität, p. 14.
[200] Cf. ibid., p. 94.
[201] Cf. **Gruner**, Wolf D., **Woyke**, Wichard, Europa-Lexikon, p. 11.
[202] Cf. ibid., p. 12.
[203] Cf. **Wagner**, Hartmut, Bezugspunkte europäischer Identität, p. 55.
[204] Cf. **Guisan**, Catherine, A political theory of identity in European integration, p. 127.
[205] Cf. **Wagner**, Hartmut, Bezugspunkte europäischer Identität, p. 58.
[206] **Cederman**, Lars-Erik, Exclusion Versus Dilution: Real or Imagined Trade-Off, in: **Cederman**, Lars-Erik, Constructing Europe's Identity. The external dimension, Boulder, CO 2001, p. 245.

ments"[207]. One of the essential premises, the definition of the *other*,[208] thus cannot be fulfilled by the criterion of territory. Subsequently, there is no lasting and solid territory an EU-identity can rely on.

However, one has also to note that Europe is "a region and an idea"[209]. Since the end of the Cold War, the European map has changed dramatically.[210] The EU has worked hard on the "twin pursuit of building up external borders while erasing internal borders"[211] while simultaneously enlarging its size.[212] Today, it has "twenty-seven member states and is due to take in Croatia"[213] in July 2013. Moreover, several Balkan States are entitled to be EU member states in the upcoming decades which would lead to an increased territory again. The reference object is always clearly defined, though. Dynamic and smart enlargement comes along with a multitude of chances and possibilities furthering integration and stability. There might not be a final idea of the EU, but this leaves its policy makers the best preconditions to sustainably and flexibly create a steady and solid entity. Its territorial incompleteness can be seen as a characteristic now.[214] However, the EU has to establish and to define its final external borders in the future[215] since "to define one's borders is to define one's identity" [216]. The component of territorial reference in order to forge an EU-identity is definitely one of the most reliable and visible ones. Its borders are defined by the external borders of its member states, but they are not meant to last forever this way. Still, EU-citizens can rely on the present territory which is legally and politically specified. Moreover, the EU member states are identifiably belonging to the EU which will especially be illustrated in the chapter on common symbols.

2. Language: The confusion of tongues

Along with territory, language ranks very highly when it comes to defining national identity which becomes relevant in the self-designation of a nation and its people's language.[217] Language enables people to differentiate between people who speak their mother tongue and

---

[207] **Hooghe**, Marc, Does Multi-level governance Reduce the Need for National Government?, in: European Political Science, 2012 (1), p. 94.
[208] Cf. **Schmitt-Egner**, Peter, Europäische Identität, p. 25.
[209] **Bohne**, Eberhard, EU and US Security Strategies, p. 13.
[210] Cf. **Herz**, Dietmar, **Jetzlsperger**, Christian, Die Europäische Union, München 2008, p. 122.
[211] **Guisan**, Catherine, A political theory of identity in European integration, p. 128.
[212] Today, the EU covers 75% of Europe, two-thirds of the European nations are member states and 4/5 of the population are EU-citizens, cf. **McCormick**, John, Understanding the European Union, p. 36 f.
[213] **Risse**, Thomas, A Community of Europeans?, p. 56.
[214] Cf. **Bohne**, Eberhard, EU and US Security Strategies, p. 7.
[215] Cf. **Hänsch**, Klaus, Perspektiven der europäischen Integration, p. 69.
[216] **Guisan**, Catherine, A political theory of identity in European integration, p. 128.
[217] E.g. German is spoken in Germany, French is spoken in France, Polish is spoken in Poland et cetera and the appellation of the population is derived from the nation's name, cf. **Wagner**, Hartmut, Bezugspunkte europäischer Identität, p. 68.

those who do not.[218] It thus fosters the genesis of national identities. The search for a commonly shared mother tongue is essential for identity discourses.[219]

The lack of a common European language cannot be ignored: it obviously restrains the communication amongst Europeans and stems the genesis of the mindset of one European people.[220] Thence, one might assume, an EU-identity "is not possible, because there is no common language that might constitute a political community"[221]. For though there are bilingual or even multilingual EU member states, their plurality cannot be compared with the degree of multilingualism in the EU.[222] The "linguistic divisions of Europe are substantial"[223] and within the concept of collective identities, every language[224] is defended as a symbol of national identity. Consequently, the majority of EU-citizens cannot communicate with the majority of EU-citizens[225] due to the lack of an official lingua franca.[226] Therefore, "all official EU documents [have to be] translated into the 23 official languages of the member states"[227], thus causing a lot of work, bureaucracy and the permanent risk of misinterpretation.

It is only recently that owing to the globalization process and the internationalization of politics, one "can actually observe an emerging common language in Europe, namely English"[228]. Its dominance increases[229] and it is slowly but inexorably becoming the lingua franca of Europe.[230] Despite the difficulties this variety of tongues may cause, the EU's "official language policy celebrates this diversity of linguistic competences"[231], regarding it as a uniqueness that must be enshrined.[232] The EU endeavors to "promote respect for linguistic and cultural differences within Europe's nation states"[233]. Multilingualism has been noted as a difficulty that cannot be equalized by any measures. Instead, it has to be perceived as a valuable heritage, fostering cross-cultural approaches, and promoting "a sense of community"[234]. Consequently,

---

[218] Cf. ibid., p. 69.
[219] Cf. **Schmale**, Wolfgang, Geschichte und Zukunft der Europäischen Identität, p. 101.
[220] Cf. **Wagner**, Hartmut, Bezugspunkte europäischer Identität, p. 88.
[221] **Risse**, Thomas, A Community of Europeans?, p. 38.
[222] Cf. **Kielmannsegg**, Peter Graf, Integration und Demokratie, p. 58.
[223] **McCormick**, John, Understanding the European Union, p. 33.
[224] According to estimates, there are 255 different laguages spoken in Europe, cf. **Wagner**, Hartmut, Bezugspunkte europäischer Identität, p. 67.
[225] Cf. **Kielmannsegg**, Peter Graf, Integration und Demokratie, p. 58.
[226] Cf. **Wagner**, Hartmut, Bezugspunkte europäischer Identität, p. 95.
[227] **McCormick**, John, Understanding the European Union, p. 33.
[228] **Risse**, Thomas, A Community of Europeans?, p. 39.
[229] Cf. **McCormick**, John, Understanding the European Union, p. 33.
[230] Cf. ibid., p. 109.
[231] **Risse**, Thomas, A Community of Europeans?, pp. 38 f.
[232] Cf. **Landais**, Joël, Identité nationale et identité européenne, http://www.sauvonsleurope.eu/identite-nationale-et-identite-europeenne/, [online] 05.10.2012.
[233] **Linklater**, Andrew, A European Civilising Process, p. 368.
[234] **Risse**, Thomas, A Community of Europeans?, p. 39.

there is not one language an EU-identity can refer to, but a multitude of languages. This unique diversity can still be a solid component of an EU-identity.

3. Legal framework and politics

Legally binding treaties are the real foundation of the EU, thus endowing it with an official and obliging character. By creating new international legal precedents and by testing them, the fundamental objectives of the EU can be implemented.[235] The EU is the result of a political campaign leading to the European Movement in the 1940s.[236] European cooperation – primarily in the frames of economy and politics – "was intended to bring prosperity and peace, and the second largely because of the first"[237] after World War II. Its formal principles were the rule of law and democracy.[238] The EU-citizens basic rights are lawfully protected through the Charter of Fundamental Rights of the European Union.[239] This modernistic approach[240] adapts ideas of socioscientific discourses. The law of the EU is enforceable through the European Court of Justice (ECJ)[241], thus guaranteeing the same degree of justice to every EU-citizen. After the Treaty of Lisbon, the EU member states can significantly influence[242] the further developments of the EU, as they set boundaries and decide on political contents. Through the implementation of a "supra-national legal system"[243], the EU has created a community governed by the rule of law. This development has been furthering the European integration sustainably,[244] enabling it to secure peace and freedom within its territory. Hence, the EU has undoubtedly accomplished forming an identity and has increased the awareness[245] through a legal framework.

European economic systems in particular have been positively impacted by advances in EU law. It is therefore one of the lasting and most stable "factors which consolidate the unity of

---

[235] Cf. **Borchardt**, Klaus-Dieter, Das ABC des Rechts der Europäischen Union, Luxemburg 2010, p. 141.
[236] **Hick**, Alan, Die Europäische Bewegung, p. 239.
[237] **Calhoun**, Craig, The Virtues of Inconsistency, p. 37.
[238] Thence, any action carried out by the EU has to cope with these two principles. Moreover it has to be the result of a democratic and lawful legitimating process, cf. **Borchardt**, Klaus-Dieter, Das ABC des Rechts der Europäischen Union, p. 31.
[239] Cf. **Dienel**, Christiane, **Overkämping**, Sabine, Der Vertrag von Lissabon und die europäische Sozialpolitik, in: **Leiße**, Olaf (Ed.), Die Europäische Union nach dem Vertrag von Lissabon, Wiesbaden 2010, p. 183.
[240] Cf. **Dienel**, Christiane, **Overkämping**, Sabine, Der Vertrag von Lissabon und die europäische Sozialpolitik, p. 190.
[241] Cf. **Jacobs**, Dirk, **Maier**, Robert, European Identity: construct, fact, fiction, p. 21.
[242] Cf. **Hänsch**, Klaus, Perspektiven der europäischen Integration, p. 74.
[243] **Jacobs**, Dirk, **Maier**, Robert, European Identity: construct, fact, fiction, p. 21.
[244] Cf. **Everling**, Ulrich, Bindung und Rahmen: Recht und Integration, in: **Weidenfeld**, Werner (Ed.), Die Identität Europas, München 1985, p. 172.
[245] **Czarny**, Raphaël, Existe-t-il und identité européenne?

European states and peoples"[246]. Cooperation amongst economic actors "is based on two principles: an objective necessity of such contacts and mutual benefit."[247] With equal rights for all kinds of businesses within one of the world's most important economic agglomeration, the EU forms a supremely strong economic unit. The process of integration on the economic and legal level is very advanced[248] – a lot more than EU-citizens might anticipate; not least because the conditions for joining the EU are subject to certain regulations within these spheres and the consequences of a membership is a successively increasing unification of law[249], viz. the compulsory adaptation of EU law. With EU law gaining access to more and more levels of people's life, their attention is gradually drawn to the EU, away from the former "exclusive, sovereign, territorial state"[250]. EU law has succeeded in becoming one of "the few fixed points on the horizon of European politics"[251] and an important identity marker for an EU-identity. The general legal framework of the EU can be described as a mélange of traditional elements, "transitory structures of renewal, and new forms of cooperation as yet to be developed"[252]. Referring to the indispensable legitimization of EU law, a political body has to be lawfully institutionalized.[253] More than that, the Europeanization of politics has to be increasingly fostered in order to prevent national-driven partiality of politicians making these very laws.[254] Within the EU, the compliance with and the protection of the rule of law are guaranteed through the direct use of EU law and its seniority.[255]

Referring to Kielmannsegg's assumptions, one can state that pertaining to the legal framework of the EU, his assumption of three kinds of communities is supported. Through the political decision-making process and potential debates, communication amongst EU member states has to take place. Consequences of EU law can be experienced and EU-citizens benefit from its favorable outcomes. Compared to other nations, the reference time is not very long. However, the EU's achievements are remarkable. Thus emphasizing the importance of a legal framework as a distinct component of an EU-identity, one cannot find a reason "why 'constitutional patriotism' could not work on the scale of Europe"[256].

---

[246] **Parkhalina**, Tatyana, Europe. The concept of a "common European home", p. 191.
[247] Ibid.
[248] **Schäfers**, Bernhard, Sozialstruktur und sozialer Wandel in Deutschland, p. 313.
[249] Cf. **Everling**, Ulrich, Bindung und Rahmen: Recht und Integration, p. 152.
[250] **Wæver**, Ole, **Kelstrup**, Morten, Europe and its nations: political and cultural identities, p. 68.
[251] **Weidendfeld**, Werner, **Janning**, Josef, After 1989: The Emerge of a new Europe, p. 30.
[252] Ibid., p. 22.
[253] Cf. **Wæver**, Ole, **Kelstrup**, Morten, Europe and its nations: political and cultural identities, p. 76.
[254] Cf. **Darnstädt**, Thomas, **Schult**, Christoph, **Zuber**, Helene, The Great Leap Forward. In Search of a United Europe, http://www.spiegel.de/international/europe/the-great-leap-forward-in-search-of-a-united-europe-a-799292.html, [online] 05.01.2013.
[255] Cf. **Borchardt**, Klaus-Dieter, Das ABC des Rechts der Europäischen Union, p. 141.
[256] **Calhoun**, Craig, The Virtues of Inconsistency, p. 39.

4. History: Experience and roots

From a historical point of view, the term of EU-identity is closely connected to the Occident as defined by Christianity. But at the same time, it is clearly separated from the *other*, the Orient. Both religious and cultural blocks required their very counterpart.[257] Despite oriental intrusions in the course of time, occidental Europe can still be defined as a coherent cultural area. In the following, two points of view will be presented, one assuming that the EU cannot rely on a common history, the other supporting the idea that there is a commonly shared history – based on the premise that an identity being constructed requires a contingent historical background.[258]

Critics of an EU-identity often use the historical fragmentation as a basic counter-argument. In their opinion, there is no European past, but a plurality of national historiographies.[259] Thence, they conclude, there is no common history an EU-identity might rely on.[260] With Europe's scattered regionalism over the centuries, it did not have the chance to develop fully European annals[261], concertedly embracing all national histories. National or regional identities could emerge due to the closeness of culture, language, and "a concrete historical context"[262]. However, the European continent was simply too vast and the means of communication too undeveloped to generate a cross-national kind of identity. Consequently, there is "no glorious European history to be proud of in the same way that British or French histories are narrated in a triumphant way"[263]. National sovereigns fostered the genesis of national identities in order to consolidate their position and to define the *other*, mostly neighboring hostile nations. Furthermore, the European nations' individual developments have produced an enormous variety of cultures, their burning national ambitions have led to unfavorable outcomes.[264] Moreover, there are very few broadly European myths. Myths are regarded as the emotional fundament of a nation[265], thus providing a commonly shared basing point for the development of an identity. Compared to the quantity of national myths, the EU can refer to two major ones only which will be mentioned in the next paragraph.

---

[257] Cf. **Heine**, Peter, Islam in Europa als Problem einer europäischen Identität, in: **Kutz**, Martin, **Weyland**, Petra (Eds.), Europäische Identität? Versuch, kulturelle Aspekte eines Phantoms zu beschreiben, Bremen 2000, p. 259.

[258] Cf. **Wagner**, Hartmut, Bezugspunkte europäischer Identität, p. 59.

[259] Cf. **Kielmannsegg**, Peter Graf, Integration und Demokratie, p. 59.

[260] Cf. **Wagner**, Hartmut, Bezugspunkte europäischer Identität, p. 63.

[261] Cf. ibid., p. 60.

[262] **Hapke**, Yvonne, Identity and Integration in Europe, p. 92.

[263] **Risse**, Thomas, A Community of Europeans?, p. 56.

[264] The cultural diversity did not only cause wars and conquests, but also initiated crusades, inquisitions, colonization, slavery, exploitation, repression and thus, was in many ways not desireable, cf. **Szyszko**, Agata, Die kulturelle Identität Europas als ideen- und begriffsgeschichtliches Konzept, p. 18.

[265] Cf. **Wagner**, Hartmut, Bezugspunkte europäischer Identität, p. 61.

Notwithstanding the fragmented past, the EU can still refer to a „common history"[266]. Every single member state's roots can be traced back to the same "historical and religious heritage"[267]. Considered as the "cradle of modern human civilization [Europe] has given birth to a variety of cultural, philosophical and social trends and forces"[268] that spread out globally. The Enlightenment has most notably changed the world,[269] rocking old structures, ancient orders, and ideas. Ancient Greece bequeathed the EU democracy and reason; the traumatic experience of the two World Wars taught Europe peace.[270] Endowed with cultural knowledge of all kinds[271], EU-citizens can doubtlessly refer to a common historical culture which can be experienced all over the Union. Thence, a feeling of togetherness simply has to be uncovered. Certainly, the regional perception and implementation might have differed, but since they originate from the same cultural spring, they still create a "sense of community"[272] amongst people. Furthermore, the belligerent European history illustrates a constant struggle for freedom.[273]

Despite the laïcité the EU feels committed to today, the mutually shared history of religion, namely Christianity, cannot be denied. Convents and universities have been exclusively maintained and organized by the Church all over Europe and provided people with education.[274] The Church's influence on politics, traditions, social lifestyle, and even the economy can hardly be estimated, although the "medieval religious unity"[275] has disappeared. Even though the EU decided to disestablish formal religious affiliations in order to prevent any religious conflicts to have political effects, religion will always play an extremely prominent role in EU-societies.[276] A prospective EU-identity and a confessional identity do not necessarily have to be mutually exclusive though.[277] Kielmannsegg's tripartite design of communities is sufficiently compliant with religion as a historical component. It fosters communication, people can experience religion if they want to and religious holidays necessarily structure their schedules, and finally, the memory of past events is mutually shared.

---

[266] **Bohne**, Eberhard, EU and US Security Strategies, p. 7.
[267] **Risse**, Thomas, A Community of Europeans?, p. 51.
[268] **Parkhalina**, Tatyana, Europe. The concept of a "common European home", p. 187.
[269] Cf. **Bifulco**, Marco, In search of an identity for Europe, p. 11.
[270] Cf. **Toussaint**, Thomas, Identité européenne: la face cachée de la crise
[271] European fine arts, its literature and music and its architecture set salient and sustainable patterns on a global level, cf. **Daun**, Åke, Cultural Diversity, in: **Daun**, Åke, **Jansson**, Sören (Eds.), Europeans. Essays on Culture and Identity, Lund 1999, p. 269.
[272] Ibid.
[273] Cf. **Szyszko**, Agata, Die kulturelle Identität Europas als ideen- und begriffsgeschichtliches Konzept, p. 19.
[274] Cf. **Schäfers**, Bernhard, Sozialstruktur und sozialer Wandel in Deutschland, p. 302.
[275] **Bifulco**, Marco, In search of an identity for Europe, p. 4.
[276] Cf. **Heine**, Peter, Islam in Europa als Problem einer europäischen Identität, p. 269.
[277] Cf. **Checkel**, Jeffrey T., **Katzenstein**, Peter J., Conclusion, p. 215.

Thirdly, nationalism is another major trait of a common European history. This political format has been generated in Europe[278] and the modern nation state is perceived as the most natural institution. Referring to Habermas' theory, a prospective EU-identity has to go beyond that of a nation state's in order to successfully be established.

One can concede that the reservoir of European myths is not very rich. Yet, its most famous myth gave the continent its name: Princess Europe was abducted by a bull, metamorphosed Greek god Zeus.[279] Another myth fostering a feeling of a common past is "pater Europae"[280]. Frankish emperor Charlemagne succeeded in uniting large parts of Europe for several decades under his reign. This historical ambition can be perceived as an early vision EU-citizens can refer to in order to find a basis for their mutual identity.

The commonly shared experiences of the Cold War[281] are another example of modern history. Today, however, EU-citizens are aware destruction caused by past quarrels.[282] Unity and peace[283] are important aspects for the genesis of an EU-identity, "constructed against the European past of wars, nationalism, and militarism as the EU 'other'"[284]. A sustainable and tailored EU identity policy should aim at creating a modern myth: The role of the EU in the modern world as a peacekeeper[285], a peacemaker, and a community.[286] Consequently, not only ancient history would be perceived as an identity marker, but particularly modern, EU-related, history. This "blending of old and new elements"[287] is a credible and reliable object of reference for EU-citizens.

5. Community: Legitimacy and control

As with all of its member states, the EU wants to be a democratic system to the core, based on a *popular* democracy.[288] The EU defines itself as a civil power – thence dependent on legitimization – which is important for its prospective political identity.[289] In times of crisis, how-

---

[278] Cf. **Wagner**, Hartmut, Bezugspunkte europäischer Identität, p. 59.
[279] Cf. ibid. p. 61.
[280] Ibid., p. 62.
[281] Cf. **Kielmannsegg**, Peter Graf, Integration und Demokratie, p. 59.
[282] Cf. **Czarny**, Raphaël, Existe-t-il und identité européenne ?
[283] Cf. **Wagner**, Hartmut, Bezugspunkte europäischer Identität, p. 66.
[284] **Risse**, Thomas, A Community of Europeans?, p. 56.
[285] Cf. **Wagner**, Hartmut, Bezugspunkte europäischer Identität, p. 66.
[286] Cf. ibid., p. 95.
[287] **Checkel**, Jeffrey T., **Katzenstein**, Peter J., Conclusion, p. 223.
[288] Cf. **Béthouart**, Bruno, L'identité européenne chez les démocrates-chrétiens : conviction, évolution, in : **Villain-Gandossi**, Christiane (Ed.), L'Europe à la recherche de son identité, Paris 2002, p. 350.
[289] **Meyer**, Thomas, Die Identität Europas, p. 196.

ever, the "democratic credibility of the European project"[290] has suffered. In order to stabilize the EU's economy[291], numerous political decisions had to be taken that seem to impose burdensome commitments on some EU-citizens more than on others. Thus, this uneven distribution of responsibilities does not seem to reflect one EU community who legitimates and controls politics as a whole[292] – and in the same breath benefits from unequal treatment. An EU community would create a public sphere which has to face numerous assignments.[293] But is there an EU community at all?

An EU *demos*, dedicated to public welfare[294], would come to effect through virtual and real networking. Thus, its role as a collective actor in the public sphere would go beyond controlling and legitimating. Unlike a European *demos*[295], an EU *demos* can be concisely defined within political, geographical, economical, and social limits and would accordingly form an EU community. The EU integration[296] aimed at creating a feeling of community amongst the member states. However, there is not one single EU *demos*[297] noticeable by now, but at least 28 different people; neither is there an EU civil society[298] nor a common public sphere[299]. Another problem is the lack of political organizations[300] on EU level. This significantly hinders the development of an EU community, since people vote for national political parties in EU elections. In addition, the aforementioned problem of multilingualism is both reason[301] for and consequence of community deficit. Communication amongst people with different mother tongues demands initiative, action, and education. One cannot assume that every EU-citizen is willing to participate in this interactive process. Over the past decades, the EU citizens' "civic engagement"[302] has even decreased. Referring to the assumption that an EU-

---

[290] **Darnstädt**, Thomas, **Schult**, Christoph, **Zuber**, Helene, The Great Leap Forward. In Search of a United Europe

[291] Cf. **Westerwelle**, Guido, Der Wert Europas, p. 92.

[292] "The notion was that ultimate authority was vested in the people, and so the legitimate ruler (or system of rule) was that which (1) served the interests of the people or (2) better yet, received the consent of the people or (3) best of all, was positively chosen or created by the people", **Calhoun**, Craig, The Virtues of Inconsistency, p. 38.

[293] Apart from controlling the political sphere, it would inform its members and shape a public opinion. Moreover, a public sphere mediates between those who govern and those who are governed, thus legitimating the political system as a whole, cf. **Wagner**, Hartmut, Bezugspunkte europäischer Identität, p. 85.

[294] Cf. **Schmitt-Egner**, Peter, Europäische Identität, p. 62.

[295] Cf. **Schmale**, Wolfgang, Geschichte und Zukunft der Europäischen Identität, p. 38.

[296] Cf. **Datler**, Georg, Europäische Identität jenseits der Demos-Fiktion, p. 59.

[297] Cf. **Wagner**, Hartmut, Bezugspunkte europäischer Identität, p. 88.

[298] Cf. **Kielmannsegg**, Peter Graf, Integration und Demokratie, p. 60.

[299] Cf. **Wagner**, Hartmut, Bezugspunkte europäischer Identität, , p. 95.

[300] Cf. **Darnstädt**, Thomas , **Schult**, Christoph, **Zuber**, Helene, Citizens of the EU. How to Forge a Common European Identity, http://www.spiegel.de/international/europe/citizens-of-the-eu-how-to-forge-a-common-european-identity-a-800775.html, [online] 05.01.2013.

[301] Cf. **Wagner**, Hartmut, Bezugspunkte europäischer Identität, p. 88.

[302] **Vogt**, Ludgera, Das Kapital der Bürger. Theorie und Praxis zivilgesellschaftlichen Engagements, Frankfurt/Main 2005, S. 147.

identity can co-exist with national or other kinds of identity, an exchange through communi-cation is an entitative component. It creates some kind of compensation[303] which is necessary to keep their own identity and to accept the *other's* nature, as well. Common traits can be no-ticed and appreciation is fostered through communication. In order to resurrect this attitude, the EU necessarily has to offer an attractive and persuading policy option which is democrati-cally legitimated to forge an EU-identity. Yet, an EU *demos* does not have to be presupposed for democratization. This process is the reason for the establishment[304] of a *demos*. Commu-nication across the EU simultaneously broach accordant issues. Thence, their belonging to an EU *family of nations* is highlighted and create identity.[305] The potential of communication is not properly transformed into a drive for the creation of identity though. Indeed, the mass me-dia possesses the two decisive characteristics that can help in this regard: contemporaneity and accordance of issues. They are able to envision[306] the EU feeling towards the addressees. However, mass media have not yet been sufficiently *Europeanized* yet. The focus of national media remains narrow,[307] and state-focused, hardly broadening its program towards a Europe-an range.

In summary, the public sphere created by an EU community is an instrument to render these benchmarks tangible.[308] Community, however, depends on auxiliary devices, e.g. standard-ized mass media, language, common symbols etc. Consequently, an EU *demos* can be gener-ated who unanimously form the EU through legitimization and control of its representatives.

6. Values: The dynamic key benchmark

Due to its historical and philosophical origins[309], Europe is considered to be a „continent of human values"[310]. It has witnessed the spirit of the pacifying Sermon of the Mount[311] as well as tyranny and devastation. A European value grid has been developed over the centuries tak-ing into consideration the lessons it had to learn. EU law consists of binding treaties of great importance[312] preserving and representing[313] these values, so they demand utmost supportive

---

[303] Cf. **Weidenfeld**, Werner, **Turek**, Jürgen, Wie Zukunft entsteht, p. 189.
[304] Cf. **Wagner**, Hartmut, Bezugspunkte europäischer Identität, p. 90.
[305] Ibid., p. 85.
[306] Cf. ibid., pp. 85 f.
[307] Cf. ibid., p. 86.
[308] Cf. ibid., p. 92.
[309] The Preamble of the Treaty of Lisbon refers to "the cultural, religious and humanist inheritance of Europe, from which have developed the universal values of the inviolable and inalienable rights of the human person, freedom, democracy, equality and the rule of law", thus esteeming a common heritage.
[310] **Bohne**, Eberhard, EU and US Security Strategies, pp. 6 and 14.
[311] Cf. **Weidenfeld**, Werner, Europa im Umbruch: Perspektiven einer neuen Ordnung des Kontinents, p. 14.
[312] Cf. **Wagner**, Hartmut, Bezugspunkte europäischer Identität, p. 71.
[313] Cf. **Schmitt-Egner**, Peter, Europäische Identität, p. 237.

legitimization for the norms are obeyed. With regard to the plurality of its member states, the EU needs to word these values, in particular the core values[314], in an understandable and meticulous manner, so they can be considered to be valuable and acceptable. The Treaty on the Functioning of the European Union (Article I-2[315]) and the latest document, the Treaty of Lisbon (Article 1a[316]), write down the EU's most decisive values thus subsuming its moral base. Thence, a peaceful and tolerant way of living together in a community is guaranteed.[317] These mutually shared values are highly appreciated and noticed in the member states. Moreover, they are an essential contribution and stimulus for a European integration which makes them one of the most important benchmarks[318] and identity markers[319] for an EU-identity.

EU citizens are part of a community based on shared values. Apart from the salient positions within the aforementioned EU treaties, this becomes obvious in three points.[320] The EU defines itself (1) through common European values[321], potential member states (2) have to respect these common values and (3) potential disesteem will be noticed due to a rapid alert system and a sanctioning mechanism. Therefore, the implementation and protection of values is guaranteed across the EU since all its member states have incorporated the canon of values. Its citizens can therefrom refer to one institution in respect of values. The universality and global omnipresence of values can undeniably be ascertained with its historical background in mind. Although Europe is the smallest continent on earth, it is unexcelled in producing lasting cultural outcomes[322], outclassing Asia, Africa and America by far. Present values[323] can exclusively be traced back to European roots.[324] It was "European values [that] have helped to make the United States of America [...] the valiant defender of freedom which she has become"[325]. Although constitutional norms have been established and institutionalized in Northern America for the first time in history, they were originally generated in Western Europe.[326]

---

[314] Cf. **Borchardt**, Klaus-Dieter, Das ABC des Rechts der Europäischen Union, pp. 21 ff.
[315] Cf. ibid. p. 21.
[316] „The Union is founded on the values of respect for human dignity, freedom, democracy, equality, the rule of law and respect for human rights, including the rights of persons belonging to minorities. These values are common to the Member States in a society in which pluralism, non-discrimination, tolerance, justice, solidarity and equality between women and men prevail."
[317] Cf. **Westerwelle**, Guido, Der Wert Europas, p. 91.
[318] Cf. **Wagner**, Hartmut, Bezugspunkte europäischer Identität, p. 94.
[319] Cf. ibid., p. 71.
[320] Cf. ibid., p. 73.
[321] For instance, one can refer to constitutional basis of the canon of values in the Preamble of the Charter of Fundamental Rights of the European Union, cf. **Weidenfeld**, Werner, **Turek**, Jürgen, Wie Zukunft entsteht, p. 179.
[322] Cf. **Gruner**, Wolf D., **Woyke**, Wichard, Europa-Lexikon, p. 19.
[323] Cf. **Schmitt-Egner**, Peter, Europäische Identität, p. 238.
[324] Cf. **Szyszko**, Agata, Die kulturelle Identität Europas als ideen- und begriffsgeschichtliches Konzept, p. 17.
[325] **Thatcher**, Margaret, A Family of Nations, p. 51.
[326] Cf. **Schmitt-Egner**, Peter, Europäische Identität, p. 235.

Thence, appraising Europe as the *cradle of values* is not an exaggerated term. Although some values passed through a dynamic modification, adapting to ever-changing conditions, their central idea has been conserved.

Even skeptics can hardly "deny that moral ideas have influenced the development of the EU"[327]. Values are essential benchmarks for legislation, policy, and social life of the EU. Their functions meet Kielmannsegg's requirements as well. Values demand communication, first in order to define them with regard to today's conditions, second to dynamically adjust them if the situation changes, third to state or even defend them against the *other*, and fourth to raise the EU-citizens' awareness in general. Furthermore, values are experienceable and tangible when one meets the *other*, and through media, who interpret and spread them in various forms.[328] Finally, dynamically changing values are remembered as people recall their past. Hence, values can be considered to be one of the most important components of a prospective EU-identity since they refer to a society's basic spine.

7. Common symbols

A community primarily defines itself through symbols its members are familiar with.[329] Thus, they can draw a line between themselves and the *other*. In case of the EU, a set of shared symbols have been consciously developed by the EU and its institutions.[330] This "Eurosymbolism"[331] represents benchmarks of a community identity.[332] In this chapter, a selection of EU symbols will be presented. Apart from the fundamental five political symbols[333] mentioned in the European Constitution, further deeply symbolic similarities will be explored.

In a first step, one has to define the term *symbol*. Most commonly, it is understood to be "a 'physical element' used to – for example – represent a political or social collectivity [...] that could be used to attach a physically apprehensible 'signifier' to a Nation, a State, or any other human collectivity"[334]. Thus, a symbol has to be tangible and – in order to be related to a political system – legitimately accepted by the addressees. More precisely, one can furthermore distinguish between civil and cultural symbol.[335] The aforementioned myths are essential

---

[327] **Linklater**, Andrew, A European Civilising Process, p. 378.
[328] Cf. **Wagner**, Hartmut, Bezugspunkte europäischer Identität, p. 77.
[329] Cf. **Herz**, Dietmar, **Jetzlsperger**, Christian, Die Europäische Union, p. 131.
[330] Cf. **Risse**, Thomas, A Community of Europeans?, p. 57.
[331] **Jacobs**, Dirk, **Maier**, Robert, European Identity: construct, fact, fiction, p. 20.
[332] Cf. **Wagner**, Hartmut, Bezugspunkte europäischer Identität, p. 78.
[333] Cf. ibid., p. 81.
[334] **Bruter**, Michael, Citizens of Europe?, p. 75.
[335] Civic symbols (e.g. elections, currency, and passport) represent the authority of an institution, cultural symbols (e.g. anthem or design of the notes) refer to the existence of a common historical and cultural EU inheritance, cf. **Bruter**, Michael, Citizens of Europe?, p. 85.

components in establishing the EU's "own being"[336] and are insofar important elements of a prospective EU-identity. The EU's five major symbols[337] pegged in the Treaty establishing a Constitution for Europe are not concluded in the Lisbon Treaty any more. Instead, a separate declaration some EU member states avow themselves to the common symbols.[338]

The flag of the EU consists of a circle of twelve yellow stars against a dark blue background "is now ubiquitous in Europe"[339], and it is "visible on public buildings, shops, and hotels throughout the EU, and omnipresent at meetings of EU leaders"[340]. Thence, it has become a potent symbol with a high recognition factor. On May 29th, 1986, it was flown for the first time in front of the Belaymont building in Brussels, flanked by the twelve flags of the member states.[341] Despite the repetitive appearance of the number twelve, the stars do not represent the member states, but refers to the idea of completeness and harmony of old European descent.[342] The circle is meant to illustrate unity, solidarity and harmony amongst the people of Europe. Due to its ubiquity the flag is a salient identity marker.

Secondly, the anthem of the Union is the *Ode to Joy* by Ludwig van Beethoven from the 9th symphony with the words by Schiller. The idea has been approved in 1972 by the European Council and put into effect in 1985.[343] The theme of the anthem concatenates[344] the idea of joy with the idea of solidarity[345]. Although it is supposed to be played without lyrics, the words are well-known and transport these ideas to the EU citizens.

Furthermore, the motto[346] of the EU, *United in Diversity*, perfectly recaps previous conclusions. Despite the cultural, linguistic, and historical diversity within the EU, its member states have voluntarily decided to unite peacefully.[347] The plurality was esteemed to be an enrich-

---

[336] **Bohne**, Eberhard, EU and US Security Strategies, p. 7.
[337] Article I-8 of the Treaty establishing a Constitution for Europe mentions the flag of the Union, the anthem of the Union, the motto of the Union, the currency of the Union and Europe Day, also cf. **Wagner**, Hartmut, Bezugspunkte europäischer Identität, pp. 78 f.
[338] Declaration 52 on the symbols of the European Union, signed by the Kingdom of Belgium, the Republic of Bulgaria, the Federal Republic of Germany, the Hellenic Republic, the Kingdom of Spain, the Italian Republic, the Republic of Cyprus, the Republic of Lithuania, the Grand-Duchy of Luxembourg, the Republic of Hungary, the Republic of Malta, the Republic of Austria, the Portuguese Republic, Romania, the Republic of Slovenia, and the Slovak Republic.
[339] **Risse**, Thomas, A Community of Europeans?, p. 57.
[340] **McCormick**, John, Understanding the European Union, p. 108.
[341] Cf. **Kommission der Europäischen Gemeinschaften**, Europäische Identität: im Symbol, im Sport…, Stichwort Europa, 1987, p. 4.
[342] **Kunzmann**, Bernd, Europa 2012, Landau/Pfalz 2012, p. 60.
[343] **Bruter**, Michael, Citizens of Europe?, p. 83.
[344] Cf. **Kunzmann**, Bernd, Europa 2012, p. 60.
[345] In reference to the lyrics, all men can become brothers.
[346] Cf. **Wagner**, Hartmut, Bezugspunkte europäischer Identität, pp. 78 f.
[347] Cf. **Kunzmann**, Bernd, Europa 2012, p. 61.

ment for the EU. Thus, it was not intended to impose some kind of artificial identity, but to forge an identity sui generis, respecting the multitude of cultural peculiarities.

Moreover, a unionwide single currency[348] is constitutionally pegged as well. 17 member states use the Euro, including three associated countries[349], and three passive users[350]. The introduction of the Euro tore down financial boundaries, it set an end to rates of exchange, and it sustainably revitalized the EU market.[351] Notwithstanding grim and emotional debates that have taken place in the forefront of the Euro and despite the partly negative and observant positions of the public, it has been one of the most stabilizing factors[352] in the past years of crisis. In the meanwhile, the Euro "has become a symbol of European integration in the daily lives of the citizens"[353]. Its ubiquity[354] creates an experienceable benchmark in everyday life. Successful integration measures such as the Euro are perceived as an everyday experience, as "one of the most significant symbols of European unity at present"[355], and thus represent an eminent component for the generation[356] of a mutually acknowledged EU-identity. Thence, the relevance of currency goes beyond the term of a mere symbol[357]; it is an identity marker.

Europe Day refers to the Schuman Declaration from May 9th, 1950 which is considered to be the hour of birth[358] of the European Union. It was celebrated for the first time in 1986, just a couple of days before the inauguration of the European flag.[359] Ever since, it is celebrated throughout the EU, gaining more and more public attention.

Apart from these five constitutionally mentioned symbols, there are various further to be explored. So, for instance, the EU symbol is to be found on every vehicle's license plate[360] across the EU. Moreover, the Council of Ministers voted for a common EU driver's license.[361] In addition, starting in 1986, national passports were decided to phase out and to be replaced by a "standardized burgundy-colored European passport bearing the words 'European community' (later: 'European Union') in the appropriate national language, and the name

---

[348] Cf. **Weidenfeld**, Werner, **Piepenschneider**, Melanie, Junge Generation und Europäische Einigung. Einstellungen – Wünsche – Perspektiven, Bonn 1990, p. 79.
[349] Monaco, San Marino and Vatican City.
[350] Kosovo, Andorra and Montenegro.
[351] Cf. **Cohn-Bendit**, Daniel, **Verhofstadt**, Guy, Für Europa!, p. 12.
[352] Cf. **Hänsch**, Klaus, Perspektiven der europäischen Integration, p. 70.
[353] **Bohne**, Eberhard, EU and US Security Strategies, p. 15.
[354] Cf. **Wagner**, Hartmut, Bezugspunkte europäischer Identität, p. 83.
[355] **Bruter**, Michael, Citizens of Europe?, p. 84.
[356] Cf. **Weidenfeld**, Werner, **Turek**, Jürgen, Wie Zukunft entsteht, p. 179.
[357] Cf. **Villain-Gandossi**, Christiane, **Berting**, Jan, L'Europe, loin de la fin de l'histoire, p. 545.
[358] Cf. **Kunzmann**, Bernd, Europa 2012, p. 61.
[359] Cf. **Kommission der Europäischen Gemeinschaften**, Europäische Identität, p. 5.
[360] Cf. **Risse**, Thomas, A Community of Europeans?, p. 57 and **Weidenfeld**, Werner, **Piepenschneider**, Melanie, Junge Generation und Europäische Einigung, pp. 78 f.
[361] Cf. **Kommission der Europäischen Gemeinschaften**, Europäische Identität, p. 8.

and coat of arms of the holder's home state"[362]. An EU passport can contribute to the establishment of an EU-identity by fostering the feeling of togetherness across the people[363] and defining the *other*. Although there is no EU capital defined[364] in any document, people colloquially refer to Brussels[365] in general. However, the state of Brussels cannot be entirely compared to the one nation state's capitals rely on. Furthermore, there is no such institution as EU memorials[366] for decisive events. Finally, the EU can finally refer to a common constitution, "the symbol of a State, or, at the very least, a sovereign political system par excellence"[367]. It has been publically discussed and democratically legitimated. Its contents led to an increased democratization.

All these symbols sustainably serve as important identity markers.[368] They are powerful enough to "influence the specific values and connotations associated with a political project by citizens and foreigners alike"[369]. They address exclusively EU-citizens and thus define the other in the utmost obvious way.[370] Kielmannsegg's requirements are fulfilled at their best. Political symbols demand communication, they are experienceable, visible, and tangible, and due to their ubiquity and their prevalence, they are constantly subject to memorization and internalization by the populace.

ii. Transnational Identity

In the past five decades, the population of the EU experienced a constant growth.[371] All these people's interests and desires have to be paid attention to when it comes to forging an EU-identity. Due to its collective nature, there is no clinical scale to measure both its existence and intensity. Indicators of an EU-identity can be defined through benchmarks and identity markers.[372]

Given the fact that a prospective EU-identity is to exist adjacent to existing national, regional, cultural, linguistic, ethnic, and many more collective identities, one can still assume that they

---

[362] **McCormick**, John, Understanding the European Union, p. 108.
[363] Cf. **Kommission der Europäischen Gemeinschaften**, Europäische Identität, p. 7.
[364] Cf. **Wagner**, Hartmut, Bezugspunkte europäischer Identität, p. 81.
[365] **Szyszko**, Agata, Die kulturelle Identität Europas als ideen- und begriffsgeschichtliches Konzept, p. 17.
[366] **Wagner**, Hartmut, Bezugspunkte europäischer Identität, p. 81.
[367] **Bruter**, Michael, Citizens of Europe?, p. 85.
[368] Cf. **Risse**, Thomas, A Community of Europeans?, p. 56.
[369] **Bruter**, Michael, Citizens of Europe? The Emerge of a Mass European Identity, Houndmills 2005, p. 77.
[370] Cf. **Wagner**, Hartmut, Bezugspunkte europäischer Identität, p. 81.
[371] Its number increased from 180 m to almost 500 m in 2010 which makes almost every eleventh human being an EU-citizen, cf. **Hänsch**, Klaus, Perspektiven der europäischen Integration, p. 71.
[372] Since 1974, the European Commission semiannually publishes an opinion research report, *Eurobarometer*, studying European identity, cf. **Wagner**, Hartmut, Bezugspunkte europäischer Identität, p. 19.

"may be more or less congruent"[373] due to largely similar or closely related identity markers. The EU's identity policy[374] has been heretofore conducted by two major aspects: the principle of subsidiarity[375] and utmost respect for the EU's cultural diversity.[376] Therefore, each member state's national identity is held in high regard since they are not supposed to be completely absorbed in the EU but to play their part by contributing to the myriad of cultures generating the *sui generis* spirit.[377] Moreover, an EU-identity "will develop in tandem with national identity"[378] in order to be generated in a transnationally acceptable an acknowledgeable way. This is another evident reason why identity can never be assumed to be static[379] and why it does not necessarily have to compete with existing identities for a hierarchical position.[380] Coexistent identities can even contribute to a more pronounced formulation of every respective one.[381] Thence, an EU-identity fosters transnational understanding, communication, and cooperation.

b. The seven pieces of a blueprint for an EU-identity

The visionary concept of a dynamic[382] EU-identity brings home the necessity that ideas have to be commonly shared[383] for they can flower out. However, the genesis of an identity demands time and dedication.[384] In case of the EU-identity, time flies! Due to global pressure[385] and ever increasing challenges, the EU cannot take another century to forge its identity. Action and initiative have become bare necessities in order to sustainably stabilize the EU. Given the fact that no EU member state can rely on an unfractured identity[386], the EU can seize the opportunity and develop an identity "as a result of dynamic and dialogical processes of

---

[373] **Calhoun**, Craig, The Virtues of Inconsistency, p. 47.
[374] The nature of an EU-identity is political since EU-citizens live together in a political structure and share a common form of action, cf. **Meyer**, Thomas, Die Identität Europas, p. 229. Due to the political intention to generate an EU-identity, cultural identities and the definition of the other are politicized, ibid., p. 233.
[375] It has "an equivalent in terms of theory of identities. It is the theory that claims that several identities can coexist, but that they are additive and based on territorial proximity", **Bruter**, Michael, Citizens of Europe?, p. 16.
[376] Cf. **Flesch**, Colette, Sport und Europäische Gemeinschaft aus Sicht der EG-Kommission, in: **Rydzy-Götz**, Marlis (Ed.), Die Europäische Gemeinschaft und der Sport, Frankfurt a.M. 1992, pp. 7 f.
[377] Cf. **Borchardt**, Klaus-Dieter, Das ABC des Rechts der Europäischen Union, p. 25.
[378] **Darnstädt**, Thomas , **Schult**, Christoph, **Zuber**, Helene, Citizens of the EU.
[379] Cf. **Herz**, Dietmar **Jetzlsperger**, Christian, Die Europäische Union, p. 130.
[380] Cf. **Bruter**, Michael, Citizens of Europe?, p. 15.
[381] **Schmitt-Egner**, Peter, Europäische Identität, p. 204.
[382] Cf. **Jacobs**, Dirk, **Maier**, Robert, European Identity, p. 15.
[383] Cf. **Datler**, Georg, Europäische Identität jenseits der Demos-Fiktion, p. 61.
[384] Cf. **Landais**, Joël, Identité nationale et identité européenne.
[385] Cf. ibid.
[386] Cf. **Körber**, Kurt A., Bergedorfer Gesprächskreis, p. 107.

situational self-construction"[387]. Societies are cultural systems who constantly pass through all kinds of changes[388] thus creating a one-of-a-kind dynamic.

Given its territorial size and its plurality of cultures, an EU-identity can most probably never draw level with national identities referring to emotions and passion[389], but it can complete people's desires. EU-citizens are not only holding Bavarian, Breton, Flemish or Basque identities, but also national identities, and cross-national linguistic identities (e.g. in South Tyrol or Alsace), hence multiple identities.[390]

The beforehand presented seven components of a prospective identity take into consideration the dynamics of the genesis as well as the coexistential character of an EU-identity. Interconnectedly transferred on EU-projects aiming at fostering a commonly shared identity, they can be seen as a blueprint for an EU-identity embodying distinctive identity markers. This blueprint's requirements should be met by any respective EU-project.

c. Advantageous pluralism and demanding necessities

Despite a common cultural inheritage, there is a paradox mélange[391] of familiarity and strangeness amongst the EU member states. As a matter of fact, "contrasts are recognized between countries"[392] and people pay remarkably less attention to similarities. For this reason, changes and differences are emphasized. An EU-identity thence has to clearly accentuate these commonly shared aspects through appropriate identity markers. It can rely on a traditional subliminal consciousness of a European identity whose idea can be traced back for centuries[393] as shown before. One major premise the genesis of an EU-identity is based on is the maintenance of national identities. Critics and opponents often produce the argument that a potential EU-identity might replace[394] or *bulldoze*[395] national identities. Contrary, protecting

---

[387] **Schubotz**, Dirk, **Svašek**, Maruška, **Miller**, Robert, **Domecka**, Markieta, Into and Out of Europe: Dynamic Insider/Outsider Perspectives, in: **Miller**, Robert, **Day**, Graham (Eds.), The Evolution of European Identities. Biographical approaches, Basingstoke 2012, p. 186.
[388] Cf. **Heine**, Peter, Islam in Europa als Problem einer europäischen Identität, p. 270.
[389] Cf. **Meyer**, Thomas, Die Identität Europas, p. 189.
[390] Cf. **Bohne**, Eberhard, EU and US Security Strategies, p. 6.
[391] Cf. **Weidenfeld**, Werner, Europa im Umbruch, p. 14.
[392] **Daun**, Åke, Cultural Diversity, p. 269.
[393] Cf. **Villain-Gandossi**, Christiane, **Berting**, Jan, L'Europe, loin de la fin de l'histoire, p. 547.
[394] Cf. **Schmale**, Wolfgang, Geschichte und Zukunft der Europäischen Identität, p. 37.
[395] Cf. **Herz**, Dietmar, **Jetzlsperger**, Christian, Die Europäische Union, p. 132.

and maintaining national identities is an absolute moral and political imperative[396] the EU has to pay regard to for the plurality's sake.

The EU-citizens' hearts have to be won (again) and their multitudinous participation has to be constantly fostered[397] in order to re-establish social acceptance. The search for a political[398] EU-identity has to be responsibly implemented together through unionwide Europeanized discourses[399] that involve the broad public. Being confronted with different and *foreign* administration, behavior, and ways to find solutions offers the opportunity for everybody to scrutinize and test one's own competences.[400] Thence, lessons learned from this kind of interactive comparison can be implemented for that the own national system can be constantly improved. Due to the EU's multicultural and multinational composition, an inexhaustible source of insights[401] dynamically fosters candidness, communication, and understanding. Thus, Europe is constantly[402] developed and reshaped "in a world of global movement"[403]. Pluralism in combination with transnational exchange hence can be a motor for improvement.

Wagner phrases four major reasons to illustrate the necessity of an EU-identity[404]. Firstly, political decisions based on majority vote are more likely to be accepted. Moreover, an EU-identity supports integration and fosters its development. Thirdly, a geographical finality in matters of boundaries is envisaged. Finally, he points out that common interests can be worded which enable EU institutions to define an EU-identity.

Apart from that, the single European market with its conditions, restrictions, and requirements produces important stimuli for growth and competitiveness.[405] Especially the single currency has led to stability in prices[406] that has never existed before. Acting as individual countries, the EU member states would never acquire a comparable position as a global actor[407] and re-

---

[396] Cf. **Toussaint**, Thomas, Identité européenne: la face cachée de la crise.

[397] Recent EU elections have experiences an ever decreasing voter turnout, although the competences of the European Parliament has been constantly enlarged, cf. **Herz**, Dietmar, **Jetzlsperger**, Christian, Die Europäische Union, p. 119.

[398] Those who are in a position to act on a political level and thus can initiate such debates are in charge, cf. **Weidenfeld**, Werner, **Janning**, Josef, After 1989: The Emerge of a new Europe, p. 29.

[399] Cf. **Lichtenstein**, Dennis, Auf der Suche nach Europa: Identitätskonstruktionen und das integrative Potential von Identitätskrisen, p. 7.

[400] Cf. **Schmitt-Egner**, Peter, Europäische Identität, p. 217.

[401] Cf. **Cohn-Bendit**, Daniel, **Verhofstadt**, Guy, Für Europa! Ein Manifest, pp. 44 f.

[402] Cf. **Riordan**, James, **Krüger**, Arnd, **Terret**, Thierry, Histoire du Sport en Europe, Paris 2004, p.15.

[403] **Schubotz**, Dirk, Svašek, Maruška, **Miller**, Robert, **Domecka**, Markieta, Into and Out of Europe, p. 185.

[404] Cf. **Wagner**, Hartmut, Bezugspunkte europäischer Identität, pp. 41 ff.

[405] Cf. **Westerwelle**, Guido, Der Wert Europas, p. 92.

[406] Cf. ibid.

[407] Cf. ibid., p. 93.

main rather irrelevant. Economically and politically united, these states are a lot stronger[408] and can thus significantly shape the future.[409] Such "challenges may concern either the content or the evaluation of identity"[410], sooner or later demand its generation.

An effective EU-identity policy does not necessarily have to define an endpoint of the EU but can refer to "the ambiguous phrase 'toward an ever closer union'"[411]. Given the necessity of respecting the member states' individual national identity, a prospective EU-identity is not the sum of these but an identity sui generis.[412] Although researchers argue that this process needs time[413], the EU would be better of acting as soon as possible. The advantageous pluralism has led to a multitude of toeholds, to concepts, and to auspicious ideas. However, it is not the time to tarry, but to initiate sustainable projects that foster an EU-identity.

---

[408] Cf. **Pagel**, Christoph, Festakt zum Tag der Deutschen Einheit. Lammert fordert ein „Wir sind Europa",
http://www.focus.de/politik/deutschland/festakt-zum-tag-der-deutschen-einheit-in-muenchen-lammert-fordert-ein-wir-sind-europa_aid_831691.html, [online] 05.01.2013.
[409] Cf. **Westerwelle**, Guido, Der Wert Europas, p. 92.
[410] **Hapke**, Yvonne, Identity and Integration in Europe, p. 101.
[411] **Fligstein**, Neil, Who are the Europeans and how does this matter for politics?, p. 132.
[412] Cf. **Herz**, Dietmar, **Jetzlsperger**, Christian, Die Europäische Union, p. 130.
[413] **Hänsch**, Klaus, Perspektiven der europäischen Integration, p. 71.

3. The European Union Sports Badge: One simple, smart, and sustainable project

Sport is an excellent instrument to initiate cross-cultural and cross-border "social interaction"[414]. Throughout the EU, it is the largest social movement[415] and benefits from its utmost positive reputation and attractive image.[416] Its prominent social role has already been recognized in the early stages of development[417]. In general, one can distinguish "four different dimensions of sport: sport for all, amateur sport, elite-amateur sport and professional sport"[418].

However, with the EU's initial nature as a mere economic community, sport has not been mentioned in the Treaty of Rome[419] and therefore has not been given an originary EU competence. In the course of time, sport in general has developed to an economic and social term[420] as well as the EU has become a community that does not refer to an economic agenda only. Sport undertakes a tremendous variety of tasks to address people that could never be pursued by public authorities to that extent.[421] Its ubiquity[422] led to a self-evident[423] perception of sport and due to its popularity, it has comprised an steadily increasing public[424]. Moreover, it has become an essential part of education, culture[425], and leisure activities[426], thus invigorating its formal and non-formal formation of the EU's human resources.[427] In addition, modern sport is altogether democratic, since it initially offers equal conditions to everyone[428] thus challenging the athletes' individual abilities. Furthermore, sport is organized through clubs, associations, and foundations, thus assuming responsibility for social engagement as a sponsor, promoter,

---

[414] **Hapke**, Yvonne, Identity and Integration in Europe, p. 95.
[415] Cf. **Tokarski**, Walter, Steinbach, Dirk, Spuren, p. 54.
[416] Cf. **Europäische Kommission**, Weißbuch Sport, Brüssel 2007, p. 4.
[417] Cf. **Danckert**, Peter, Kraftmaschine Parlament, p. 230.
[418] **García**, Borja, The Governance of European Sport, p. 35.
[419] Cf. **Danckert**, Peter, Kraftmaschine Parlament, p. 230.
[420] Cf. **Kepper**, Christophe de, Die Europäische Union und der Sport, p. 1.
[421] Cf. **Danckert**, Peter, Kraftmaschine Parlament, p. 261.
[422] Cf. **Markovits**, Andrei S., Sport: Motor und Impulssystem für Emanzipation und Diskriminierung, Wien 2011, p. 12.
[423] Cf. **Küchenmeister**, Daniel, **Schneider**, Thomas, Sport ist Teilhabe, Aus Politik und Zeitgeschichte, 2011 (16-19), p. 7.
[424] Cf. ibid., p., 5.
[425] Cf. **Europäische Kommission**, Die Europäische Union und der Sport, Brüssel 1996, p. 4.
[426] Cf. **Europäische Kommission**, Weißbuch Sport, p. 2.
[427] Cf. ibid., p. 5.
[428] Cf. **Markovits**, Andrei S., Sport, p. 25.

and instrument.[429] "Good governance"[430] is a major requirement for sport associations can act autonomously and self-regulating.

The principle of subsidiarity[431] has also to be paid regard to when it comes to any EU actions in the field of sport. It can only interfere if the member states do not implement commonly agrees upon objectives in a satisfiable manner. Yet, as long as sport is an economic and social issue, the EU[432] has the competence to join in lawfully. The implementation of the EU White Paper on Sport illustrated though that EU sport governance[433] could have a significant impact[434] on several realms. Any EU policy targeting at increasing the awareness for an EU-identity should "tackle present problems in a practical way"[435]. EU-citizens expect policy suggestions drawn from life, most favorably encouraging an interactive process, and ultimately designed in a creative[436] and visionary way.

In this third section, the project of a European Sports Badge (EUSB) will be presented as a practical sample to foster the genesis of an EU-identity. It does not demand a giant apparatus of administration. Instead, it is smartly designed, targeting the EU-citizens as a whole through popular sports that do not demand unique abilities or extensive training. Moreover, the EUSB is based on the premise of sustainability; its requirements can be dynamically adjusted to new sports and encourage regular participation. Subsequently, the EU-identity blueprint will be tested. In two concluding chapters, favorable side effects of this project will be presented and the institutionalization of Europeanization through the EUSB will be discussed.

a. Popular sports – literally favorable

In 1995, the EU launched the program *Eurathlon*[437] in order to foster various sports. It was supposed to target EU-citizens and to foster communication and a healthy lifestyle through sport. However, administrative restrictions and requirements make it rather difficult and opaque to apply for this program.

---

[429] Cf. **Küchenmeister**, Daniel, **Schneider**, Thomas, Sport ist Teilhabe, Aus Politik und Zeitgeschichte, 2011 (16-19), p., 5.
[430] **Europäische Kommission**, Mitteilung zum Sport (2011), p. 14.
[431] Cf. **Kepper**, Christophe de, Die Europäische Union und der Sport, pp. 2 f.
[432] Cf. **Flesch**, Colette, Sport und Europäische Gemeinschaft aus Sicht der EG-Kommission, p. 8.
[433] Sport governance can be defined as an active designing and regularization of sport based on the idea to create stable futurity. Moreover, it describes a subsidiary support of authorities in order to foster development and sponsorship for the individual and the common welfare, cf. **Danckert**, Peter, Kraftmaschine Parlament, p. 19.
[434] Cf. **Europäische Kommission**, Mitteilung zum Sport (2011), p. 4.
[435] **Thatcher**, Margaret, A Family of Nations, p. 53.
[436] Cf. **Cohn-Bendit**, Daniel, **Verhofstadt**, Guy, Für Europa!, p. 43.
[437] Cf. **Europäische Kommission**, Die Europäische Union und der Sport, pp. 4 f.

Modern sport and its various events have been originated in Europe during the past two centuries.[438] Due to mass media coverage, the economic configuration of sport, and more net leisure that can be used to actively take exercise, sport has become a mass phenomenon.[439] Physical exercise and personal fitness are nowadays well-respected and truly popular.

Popular sports in particular play an important role. Its non-profit orientation and its focus on creating a felicitous and fulfilling recreational activity distinguish this kind of sports from professional sports. Its integrative potential can hardly be grasped[440] and attach great importance to it. When working out, people surmount national, cultural, gender, and even physical differences. One can experience sport either actively as an athlete or passively as a spectator.[441] Thence, popular sports are an effective instrument for cross-cultural communication not least because of its nonverbal, universal, and culturally neutral nature.[442] Depending on how a person individually perceives sport[443], one can make it one of their personal identity markers. Most favorably, if one takes exercise for all his life[444], this identity marker will be permanent. Thence, the protection of unity in diversity[445] will be proficiently animated through sports governance with the focus on popular sports.

i. Professional sports in any spotlight

Not only with regard to media coverage, but also relating to EU sports governance, one can note that the focus is in either case on professional sports. The European model of sport is "a systematic configuration characterized by a multi-level, pyramidal and hierarchical structure of governance that runs from the international federations down to the national federations and the clubs"[446]. The vast majority of EU-citizens are not involved in these higher hierarchies. World-class and top-class sports are characterized by an enormous degree of interna-

---

[438] Cf. **Riordan**, James, **Krüger**, Arnd, **Terret**, Thierry, Histoire du Sport en Europe, p.13.
[439] Cf. **Kommission der Europäischen Gemeinschaften**, Europäische Identität, p. 9.
[440] Cf. **Danckert**, Peter, Kraftmaschine Parlament, p. 236.
[441] Cf. **Europäische Kommission**, Die Europäische Union und der Sport, p. 1.
[442] Cf. **Bröskamp**, Bernd, Glokalisierte Körper – Sport, Habitus und transnationale soziale Räume, in: **Blecking**, Diethelm, **Gieß-Stüber**, Petra (Eds.), Sport bewegt Europa. Beiträge zur interkulturellen Verständigung, Baltmannsweiler 2006, p. 120.
[443] Cf. **Stelter**, Reinhard, Du bist wie dein Sport, p. 176.
[444] Cf. **Richter**, Christiane, Konzepte für den Schulsport in Europa. Bewegung, Sport und Gesundheit, Aachen 2006, p. 277.
[445] Cf. **Danckert**, Peter, Kraftmaschine Parlament, p. 236.
[446] **García**, Borja, The Governance of European Sport, p. 39.

tionality[447]. Due to the popularity of their athletes, they become parts of global cultural industry.[448]

Moreover, professional sports are an utmost important economic factor[449], so it embraces issues such as the right to broadcast, advertising, sport equipment, gambling, journalism etc. Due to the growing popularity, this branch keeps on growing, thus providing new jobs.[450] Thence, the effects of professional sports are considered to be compelling and beneficial, and "a controlled commercialization of sport seems to be winning the debate"[451].

For the individual, professional sports have a set of detrimental influences with regard to the development of their identity. Norms, values, structure, and organization of the system[452] are obligatory and predetermined and leave little space for alternatives to the athletes. It overemphasizes economic aspects and doubtlessly has polarizing effects. Moreover, negative events such as doping scandals appeals "governing bodies to tackle widespread doping practices in sport"[453]. Thence, major parts of the EU White Paper on Sport[454] deal with the task to create a sustainable organization of sport, to initiate anti-doping policy guidelines, and to establish sagacious sports governance.

ii. A dwarfed section

Unlike professional sports, popular sports are hardly ever subject to public debates. Although sport's potential has been acknowledged, the EU mainly focuses on professional sports due to its interdependence with the economic and the gambling sector.[455] It legitimately aimed at creating union-wide mechanisms of control and jurisdiction[456], thus providing comparable conditions for top-class sport. In the mid-1980ies, the EU started sponsoring spectacular[457] sport events financially. Public sports remained a sector that did not receive consideration.

Despite the rise of significance, steady politicization of sports, and newly created international sport meetings[458], the EU has still not developed a comprehensive political sport structure,

---

[447] For instance, national ballet *équipes*, big soccer teams, and other world-class teams are composed of international professional athletes, cf. **Bröskamp**, Bernd, Glokalisierte Körper, p. 128.
[448] Cf. **Bröskamp**, Bernd, Glokalisierte Körper, p. 129.
[449] Cf. **Europäische Kommission**, Die Europäische Union und der Sport, p. 1.
[450] Cf. **Europäische Kommission**, Mitteilung zum Sport (2011), p. 11.
[451] **García**, Borja, The Governance of European Sport, p. 47.
[452] Cf. **Stelter**, Reinhard, Du bist wie dein Sport, pp. 181 f.
[453] **García**, Borja, The Governance of European Sport, p. 29.
[454] Cf. **Europäische Kommission**, Weißbuch Sport, pp. 13 ff.
[455] Cf. **Kepper**, Christophe de, Die Europäische Union und der Sport, p. 6.
[456] Cf. ibid. p. 5.
[457] Cf. **Danckert**, Peter, Kraftmaschine Parlament, p. 230.
[458] Cf. **Riordan**, James, **Krüger**, Arnd, **Terret**, Thierry, Histoire du Sport en Europe, p.13.

49

embracing all dimensions of sport – not just the most profitable one. Thence, sport could make a specific contribution to the envisaged *Europe of citizens* program[459]. The accompanying document of the White Paper on Sport, action plan *Pierre de Coubertin*, also suggests fostering this program through popular sports.[460] It is about time to target concrete policy plans implementing non-profit, leisure, and popular sports, so these are no longer a dwarfed section within EU policy. The favorable impact of popular sports[461] can no longer be ignored nor denied.

b. The project: EUSB: Compilation and objectives

The educative and formative nature of sport in general and its manifold interdependences with numerous domains foster the development of individual and collective identities (in particular through team sports).[462] EU-citizens across all boards share an interest in sport. The European Commission is conscious of the significant role it can take in bringing Europe closer to its citizens[463] since it addresses people of all nations, all ages, and all backgrounds.[464] Giving EU-citizens of different nations the chance to meet and to interact creates some kind of corporate feeling[465] that remarkably contributes to the generation of an EU-identity.

EU projects on popular sports policy have to meet several requirements. First and foremost, their design has to be sustainable[466] and long-term oriented. The EU objective target[467] – the development towards hinder ever closer union – has to be taken into consideration as well. Moreover, it must not drag existing national projects[468] in order to stick to the principle of subsidiarity, but rather complete them. Furthermore, once the focus is swiveled away from well-organized and economic-based competitive sports to popular sports[469], one has to respect that (1) there are enormous differences in the function of sports clubs in the member states[470]

---

[459] Cf. **Danckert**, Peter, Kraftmaschine Parlament, p. 230.
[460] Proposal n° 11, cf. **Europäische Kommission**, Weißbuch Sport, Aktionsplan Pierre de Coubertin, Brüssel 2007, p. 3
[461] Particularly people's wellbeing, health, education, and recreational activities are sustainably affected. Moreover, integration of all kinds and maintenance of quality of life are fostered, cf. **Tokarski**, Walter, Europa in Bewegung, p. 6.
[462] Cf. **Küchenmeister**, Daniel, **Schneider**, Thomas, Sport ist Teilhabe, p. 8.
[463] Cf. **Europäische Kommission**, Weißbuch Sport, p. 2.
[464] Ibid., p. 3.
[465] Cf. **Weidenfeld**, Werner, **Piepenschneider**, Melanie, Junge Generation und Europäische Einigung, p. 32.
[466] Cf. **Danckert**, Peter, Kraftmaschine Parlament, p. 21.
[467] Cf. **Hansen**, Hans, Europa wächst zusammen, p. 5.
[468] Cf. **Danckert**, Peter, Kraftmaschine Parlament, p. 26.
[469] Cf. **Europäische Kommission**, Weißbuch Sport, p. 3.
[470] Cf. **Tokarski**, Walter, Steinbach, Dirk, Spuren, p. 159.

and (2) people might not want to join a sports club just for the EU's sake[471] but exercise on their own. Any suggestion must be implementable and comprehensible for every member state. With sport offering something to hang on and to get orientation from, policies have to be thoughtfully formulated with regard to the important role of sport.[472] Finally, in order to address all EU-citizens, one has to create policy projects with regard to national mannerisms of sport – within a plurality of countries[473], the emphasis on specific sports might differ and specific national sports are perceived to be an important part of national culture. Taking these requirements into account will enable the EU to foster increasing social interaction while preserving national peculiarities[474] through target-oriented policy projects. A mutually acknowledged EU-identity can be significantly promoted through explicit EU projects.

One potential project can be a European Union Sports Badge (EUSB). Its open-ended and thus sustainable conception and its emphasis on inspiring every EU-citizen to exercise though popular sports mark the uniqueness and novelty of this project. Referring to familiar symbols and the idea of consistency, it demands twelve athletic performances in different sports. These should be achieved annually and be approved by certified trainers as they are engaged in sports clubs across the EU. However, a membership in a sports club shall not be mandatory. Performance requirements and instructions for the trainers should be subsumed in an adequate booklet which has to be available for everyone. Once an EU-citizen has performed a discipline, they will be given documented evidence. No one is obliged to complete the EUSB in the very same sports club. Due to its EU nature, it can be earned in every member state, thus encouraging travel, exchanges, and cross-cultural communication. In order to meet the requirement of mirroring the plurality of nations, national sports are explicitly to be embodied in the list of sports. Thus, cross-cultural understanding will be fostered and potentially, the EUSB sparks interest in new and foreign sports. Most importantly, every EU-citizens' performance will be recognized by the end of the year and their efforts will be celebrated with a badge ceremony.

At first, sports clubs, school, universities, administrative organizations, and armed forces in particular shall be encouraged to take and promote this athletic challenge for its word can spread. Yet it addresses every single EU-citizen! The introduction of the EUSB has to be accompanied by a union-wide campaign promoting sport in general, as well as a healthy life-

---

[471] Cf. **Keltek**, Tayfun, Sport als Mittel zur Integration, in: **Blecking**, Diethelm, **Gieß-Stüber**, Petra (Eds.), Sport bewegt Europa. Beiträge zur interkulturellen Verständigung, Baltmannsweiler 2006, p. 64.
[472] Cf. **Keltek**, Tayfun, Sport als Mittel zur Integration, p. 62.
[473] Cf. **Richter**, Christiane, Konzepte für den Schulsport in Europa, p. 285.
[474] Cf. **Herz**, Dietmar, **Jetzlsperger**, Christian, Die Europäische Union, p. 132.

style, and other favorable side effects. In order to make the project easily acceptable to sports clubs, its bureaucratic appendix has to be as small as possible. Thence, a standardized folded leaflet issued and provided by the EU in which performances can be written in and certified is most suitable to document the athletic achievements. Once the EUSB is completed, it can be sent to DG EAC where it will be recorded. By the end of the year, the badges will be sent to either a sports club or – if the EU-citizen is not a member – to a private address. Detailed planning is subject to entitled councils and representatives.

The badge itself shall be designed with reference to the EU symbols again. Thus, it should be composed of the flag and the lettering *EUSB* below. Moreover, it shall be conferred with a certificate appreciating and documenting the athlete's performance. The costs for the badges, the printing, and postage are at the expense of the EU and will be comparably low with regard to the enormous expenses for top-class sports sponsorship. Apart from this advantageous financial aspect, the administration required is already at hand. The production of the booklets and the launch of the campaign will cause an increased effort in the beginning, but once the project is established, its administrative tasks do not demand a big staff. The outcomes, the positive effects on people's health, and in particular their perceptions of the EU, however, are priceless and inestimable.

c. Testing the EU-identity blueprint

The EUSB project aims at purposefully contributing to the genesis, the implementation, and the fostering of a mutually acknowledged and experienced EU-identity. Therefore, it has to meet the requirements of the blueprint developed above, viz. the components have to be sufficiently fulfilled. The EU-identity "is a political construction project undertaken by [...] supranational elites"[475] and respects all its citizens' backgrounds, whether they are social, economical, cultural, or historical.[476] Sport's capability to forge close links[477] amongst people is beyond dispute. The following seven sections will test the EU-identity blueprint step by step.

i. Territory

A smart EU-identity policy project has to connect citizens to a specific territory. Given the possibility to acquire the EUSB in every EU member state, the territory of validity is clearly

---

[475] **Checkel**, Jeffrey T., **Katzenstein**, Peter J., The politicization of European identities, p. 3.
[476] Cf. **Tokarski**, Walter, Steinbach, Dirk, Spuren, p. 10.
[477] Cf. **Küchenmeister**, Daniel, **Schneider**, Thomas, Sport ist Teilhabe, p. 8.

defined. The reference to the EU per se sets the limits. EU-citizens thus can rely on the sum to territories of the member states. Moreover, the EUSB allows a clear differentiation between the EU-citizens and the *other*, since the latter cannot develop a sense of community amongst EU member states.

ii. Language

The discrepancy between the plurality of languages and the idea of a united Europe can be vanquished through the EUSB project: sport speaks all languages[478] due to its nonverbal nature. It does not palpably refer to a specific nation or language but unleashes cross-border, cross-cultural, and cross-linguistic powers.[479] Thus, the EUSB could sustainably contribute to the genesis of an EU-identity and create a sense of community amongst EU-citizens.

iii. Legal framework

The third component of the blueprint of a prospective EU-identity is very important for the legitimate and lawful implementation of the EUSB project. It respects the member states' subsidiarity and simply offers another opportunity to do sports in a non-profit way. In this connection, the EU can refer to the Treaty establishing a Constitution for Europe[480] which envisages the development of a European dimension of sport.

The Treaty of Lisbon concretizes this idea and claims a "promotion of European sporting issues, while taking account of the specific nature of sport"[481]. As mentioned before, efforts on the level of sports governance are relatively new, but their future role has to be shaped at present. The EUSB would be launched on the basis of a decision of the European Commission, hammered out by the respective council beforehand.

iv. History

Present perceptions emanate from templates of memory. Within the EU, the citizens use different templates to interpret their past.[482] A sustainable EU-identity policy has to aim at creating an EU-template by launching projects that even perceptions of EU-citizens and that is

---

[478] Cf. **Hansen**, Hans, Europa wächst zusammen, p. 5.
[479] Cf. **Tokarski**, Walter, Europa in Bewegung, p. 6.
[480] Article III-282 g, cf. **Amt für amtliche Veröffentlichungen der Europäischen Gemeinschaften**, Vertrag über eine Verfassung für Europa, Brüssel 2005, p. 133.
[481] Treaty of Lisbon, Article 149 I.
[482] Cf. **Kielmannsegg**, Peter Graf, Integration und Demokratie, p. 59.

exclusively EU-labeled.[483] Since its foundation, the EU has already written its own history, and in order to create an ever closer union, the efforts to establish an EU-historiography constantly have to be increased. In the sector of sport, the EUSB could successfully contribute.

v. Community

A sports project such as the EUSB offers unique possibilities of participation.[484] EU-citizens can either acquire the badge, or they can contribute as a trainer conducting the documentation. The EUSB "thereby helps to foster active citizenship"[485]. Given its legitimized character as an official EU-project, it will be perceived as a common venture. A simple, comprehensible, and interactive initiative addresses all EU-citizens as an EU *demos*. Moreover, the chance to take part in the project can be seized union-wide and is not narrowed down to one nation. Thence, curious EU-citizens are likely to experience the feeling of a community once they take the EUSB in another EU member state. Accordingly, this project can be grasped as a distinct incitement for an EU-identity.

vi. Values

One does not necessarily have to analyze the EU's most noble values when it comes to questioning the EUSB's impact. The domain of sport is certainly embedded in this set of values, but its outcome of specifically social values goes beyond. It can contribute to the procurance of ideal values[486], viz. ambition, discipline, assistance, etc. These values are not mere sport values, but profoundly impact various areas of life. However, their merit is hard to grasp. Values are the spine of a community and policy projects should definitely aim at strengthening and stabilizing this set of values. Due to the EUSB's favorable effect on values, it is an effective instrument to foster an EU-identity.

vii. Common symbols

With the EUSB, a new EU symbol is being generated. Its recognition value and its potential spread and visibility endow it with an enormous potential to forge an EU-identity. Furthermore, the EUSB will be a well-respected accolade since it has to be earned through athletic

---

[483] Cf. ibid., p. 60.
[484] Cf. **Küchenmeister**, Daniel, **Schneider**, Thomas, Sport ist Teilhabe, p. 8.
[485] **European Commission**, White Paper on Sport, p. 2.
[486] Cf. **Tokarski**, Walter, Europa in Bewegung, p. 6.

performance and endurance. Thence, it does not only have a tangible value, but also an ideal one. An efficient EU sports policy is supposed to originate its own identity markers that emphasize EU-citizens' solidarity with the EU.

d. Side effects

The increasingly impenetrable obscurity of the entire system causes disenchantment[487] with the concept of the EU amongst EU-citizens. Through a popular and comprehensible project such as the EUSB, this weariness can be remarkably reduced. The EU has to present itself in a more individual and self-contained way in order to meet its citizens' desires[488] and in order to sustainably define its unity. Linking political objectives and sports policy can be "seen as a cooperation-enhancing mechanism"[489], thus strengthening a common identity and fostering friendship[490] amongst EU member states. In addition, various spillover effects can be observed. They are "enduring features of policy making in the EU"[491] and can contribute to an *ever closer union* in positive way.[492] Hereinafter, a selection of six favorable side effects will be presented that come with the introduction of the EUSB.

First, encountering various kinds of sports, EU-citizens get to know their own physical limits. Thence, accompanied by an anti-doping campaign, their awareness of the danger and illegality will significantly be raised.[493] The public trivialization of this issue demands broader and comprehensive projects. Therefore, the EUSB can contribute to promote pure and legal physical performance in cooperation with anti-doping organizations.

Moreover, one has to take into consideration the evidently favorable aspects of sport for one's health[494] and prevention of diseases that physical exercise brings.[495] With regard to an increasingly ageing EU-population, sport can reduce the risk of dementia.[496] Social phenomena such as stress or burnout can also be relieved through physical exercise;[497] furthermore, regu-

---

[487] Cf. **Danckert**, Peter, Kraftmaschine Parlament, p. 236.
[488] Cf. **Weidenfeld**, Werner, **Piepenschneider**, Melanie, Junge Generation und Europäische Einigung, p. 67.
[489] **Cederman**, Lars-Erik, Exclusion Versus Dilution: Real or Imagined Trade-Off, p. 236.
[490] Cf. **Weidenfeld**, Werner, **Piepenschneider**, Melanie, Junge Generation und Europäische Einigung, p. 68.
[491] **McCormick**, John, Understanding the European Union, p. 142.
[492] Cf. **Cederman**, Lars-Erik, Exclusion Versus Dilution: Real or Imagined Trade-Off, p. 236.
[493] Cf. **Danckert**, Peter, Kraftmaschine Parlament, p. 236.
[494] Cf. **Keltek**, Tayfun, Sport als Mittel zur Integration, p. 62.
[495] E,g, obesity, adiposity, cardiovascular diseases, diabetes, cancer etc. can be effectively and consistently be fought, cf. **Europäische Kommission**, Weißbuch Sport, p. 4 and **Danckert**, Peter, Kraftmaschine Parlament, p. 290.
[496] Cf. **Danckert**, Peter, Kraftmaschine Parlament, p. 291.
[497] Cf. ibid., p. 288.

lar and moderate cardio exercise[498] positively influences the cardio system. Thence, prospectively increasing social insurance contributions can be contained[499] if more people decide to do sports. In addition, it fosters a more active and healthier lifestyle[500], thus improving people's satisfaction. Once the EUSB has been established union-wide and is carried out by habit and *tradition*, especially young EU-citizens will experience important pedagogic orientation and guidance.[501]

Following up, the EUSB can make a beneficial contribution to people's personality development. Principles[502] such as abiding by the rules, fairness, respecting other athletes, solidarity, and discipline can be communicated and demonstrated through sport – not only team sports[503], but also individual sports have this positive impact. Sports clubs in general are places of communication[504] by bringing likeminded people together.

Furthermore, sport is an ideal medium to prevent or fight violence and intolerance[505] at the roots, thus leading EU-citizens the way to a peaceful and equal way of living together.[506] Children, women[507] and migrants[508] can experience the feeling of community in a sports club and volunteering trainers[509] make a valuable contribution to social integration and civil engagement. Disabled people[510] are also given the chance to celebrate personal physical successes. Thence, social inclusion will be upvalued to a new level. Consequently, one of the utmost salient side effects of the EUSB is its contribution to a socially closer integrative society.[511]

In addition, an increased interest in sport leads to more demand of sports merchandise, thus prospectively creating new jobs.[512] It is not top-class sports' products that will be purchased, but high-quality leisure activity clothing, shoes, and equipment enabling one to physically exercise in a moderate and healthy way.

---

[498] Cf. ibid.
[499] Cf. **Europäische Kommission**, Mitteilung zum Sport (2011), p. 6.
[500] **Richter**, Christiane, Konzepte für den Schulsport in Europa, p. 279.
[501] Cf. **Danckert**, Peter, Kraftmaschine Parlament, p. 25.
[502] Cf. **Europäische Kommission**, Weißbuch Sport, p. 7.
[503] Cf. **Keltek**, Tayfun, Sport als Mittel zur Integration, p. 62.
[504] Cf. **Danckert**, Peter, Kraftmaschine Parlament, p. 261.
[505] Cf. **Europäische Kommission**, Mitteilung zum Sport (2011), p. 9.
[506] Cf. **Keltek**, Tayfun, Sport als Mittel zur Integration, p. 64.
[507] Cf. **Europäische Kommission**, Mitteilung zum Sport (2011), p. 8.
[508] Cf. **Bröskamp**, Bernd, Glokalisierte Körper, p. 120.
[509] **Europäische Kommission**, Mitteilung zum Sport (2011), p. 6.
[510] **Danckert**, Peter, Kraftmaschine Parlament, p. 281.
[511] Cf. **Europäische Kommission**, Weißbuch Sport, p. 7.
[512] Cf. **Europäische Kommission**, Die Europäische Union und der Sport, p. 3.

Finally, one can certainly discover favorable side effects with regard to an increasing security. With water sports definitely being on the EUSB-list of possible disciplines, especially children's ability to swim will be fostered. Consequently, deadly incidents (drowning) could be prevented. Even adults might feel encouraged to learn swimming if they have not done so far. Every individual's awareness of their own body and physical capability will be increased remarkably.

e. Institutionalizing Europeanization

Within the EU, different nationalities separate people, but the EU unites them.[513] However, due to its complex construction,[514] the average EU-citizen can hardly decode the scheme. Besides, the "deficiency of political courage"[515] of EU-representatives decelerates the process towards an ever closer union. The current crisis demands more than ever efficient, practical projects, politicizing quotidian issues[516] in order to win people's hearts and minds.

Thence, Europeanization has to be institutionalized. Since the meaning of this term is not fixed,[517] an optional definition shall be developed hereafter. First, it doubtlessly refers to an increasing importance of EU-cooperation, eventually leading to "a state-like European Union, connecting the process to the process of European integration"[518].

Moreover, its dynamic[519] and process-related nature[520] neither define one final objective nor do they map the road. Europeanization describes the "development of a sense of being European"[521] and thus, it is closely connected to the genesis of an EU-identity within an EU *demos* through social and political interaction. Mechanisms to meet union-wide political problems[522] have to be Europeanized, taking into consideration the plurality of origins problems may come from. A sustainable and smart process is supposed to "seek to embrace and to extend the values of liberalism, pluralism, tolerance, rationality and human dignity"[523]. The degree of

---

[513] Cf. **Cohn-Bendit**, Daniel, **Verhofstadt**, Guy, Für Europa!, p. 64.

[514] Cf. **Herz**, Dietmar, **Jetzlsperger**, Christian, Die Europäische Union, p. 119.

[515] **Parkhalina**, Tatyana, Europe. The concept of a "common European home", p. 196.

[516] **Checkel**, Jeffrey T., **Katzenstein**, Peter J., The politicization of European identities, p. 2.

[517] Cf. **Wæver**, Ole, **Kelstrup**, Morten, Europe and its nations: political and cultural identities, p. 62.

[518] Ibid.

[519] **Checkel**, Jeffrey T., **Katzenstein**, Peter J., The politicization of European identities, p. 9.

[520] **McCormick**, John, Understanding the European Union, p. 141.

[521] **Wæver**, Ole, **Kelstrup**, Morten, Europe and its nations, p. 62.

[522] Cf. **Weidenfeld**, Werner, Europa im Umbruch, p. 14.

[523] **Arter**, David, The Politics of European Integration in the Twentieth Century, Cambridge 1993, p. 276.

institutionalization of Europeanization defines EU policy in the future[524] and consequently the success of the EU project.

EU-citizens have to be aware that a stronger European identity does not weaken them, but strengthens[525] member states as well as the EU as an entity. It demands the EU-citizens' willingness to network[526] and to cooperate. This attitude can be remarkably influenced through substantial and comprehensible EU policy institutionalizing Europeanization.

---

[524]Cf. **McCormick**, John, Understanding the European Union, p. 141.
[525] Cf. **Westerwelle**, Guido, Der Wert Europas, p. 90.
[526] Cf. **Schmale**, Wolfgang, Geschichte und Zukunft der Europäischen Identität, p. 182.

Conclusion: The Bare Necessities of Life will Come to You

The question[527] about an EU-identity and the search for a reliable definition have become a discernible trend[528] in sciences. From the start, this increased interest in a way proves the necessity of looking into this issue further. The political project of a European Union can only succeed if its development goes beyond mere political necessities.[529] Thence, apart from integration on a political level, efforts have to be intensified in order to foster closer social integration. This is a major requirement for a commonly acknowledged EU-identity. However, these efforts have to be made on the premise of the EU's pluralism[530] – since the EU is a composition sui generis who cannot just impose a prospective identity "at the expense of nationality"[531]. An EU-identity has to be the result of collective debate. National identities will neither disappear[532] nor will they be replaced[533]. Each member has to be allowed, even to be encouraged, "to maintain its own identity"[534], thus enriching the EU and legitimating[535] its common identity.

A further theory says that national identities evolve a vindictive position the more nation states open to the EU.[536] Moreover, the feeling of belonging to the EU is still emerging and differing developmental stages of this bonding can be observed.[537] The process of Europeanization has to be fostered with caution. Still generating an EU-identity is necessary and the clock is ticking with regard to the multitude of challenges the EU has to face, these challenges demand mutually driven close cooperation. No individual member state will be able to cope with them on its own.[538] Consequently, an EU-identity is also a desirable object for every nation in the EU. Great value has to be set on expounding the possibility of a duality: national identities can peacefully coexist with an EU-identity.[539]

The vision[540] of an EU without borders, offering the freedom of movement, and ultimately a peaceful Europe can into being if its people develop a commonly acknowledged EU-identity,

---

[527] Cf. **Risse**, Thomas, A Community of Europeans?, p. 37.
[528] Cf. **Szyszko**, Agata, Die kulturelle Identität Europas als ideen- und begriffsgeschichtliches Konzept, p. 11.
[529] Cf. ibid. p. 22.
[530] Cf. **Bifulco**, Marco, In search of an identity for Europe, p. 28.
[531] **Arter**, David, The Politics of European Integration in the Twentieth Century, p. 276.
[532] Cf. **Herz**, Dietmar, **Jetzlsperger**, Christian, Die Europäische Union, p. 130.
[533] Cf. **Bohne**, Eberhard, EU and US Security Strategies, p. 13.
[534] **Thatcher**, Margaret, A Family of Nations, p. 49.
[535] Cf. **Kielmannsegg**, Peter Graf, Integration und Demokratie, p. 61.
[536] Cf. **Berting**, Jan, **Braak**, Hans van de, L'identité culturelle de la "Grande Europe", p. 45.
[537] Cf. **Villain-Gandossi**, Christiane, **Berting**, Jan, L'Europe, loin de la fin de l'histoire, p. 549.
[538] Cf. **Westerwelle**, Guido, Der Wert Europas, p. 90.
[539] Cf. **Wæver**, Ole, **Kelstrup**, Morten, Europe and its nations, p. 77.
[540] Cf. **Weidenfeld**, Werner, Europa im Umbruch, p. 17.

if they have the chance to interact, and to meet each other.[541] Interconnectedness between EU integration, "a clear and decisive impact for support for EU membership"[542], and an EU-identity can be stated. The more the EU fosters integration and modernization[543] of its member states, the more its citizens are likely to develop a positive attitude towards the EU and to collectively generate an EU-identity.

The greatest chance of all, however, is the fact that there is "no unified storyline"[544]. So, despite several obvious identity markers, policy makers have the freedom to design a prospective EU-identity in the most reasonable and productive way possible. The noble project of a united Europe never "had so much clarity as it does today"[545], so much impact, and so much encouragement. The process of Europeanization accompanies the genesis of an EU-identity, thus sustainably involving every EU-citizen.

So far, sport has taken in the role as poor cousin[546] in EU policy, at least non-profit popular sports. Improvements and efforts to foster its role have hitherto been related to economic benefit and tax revenue. This study has illustrated the relevance of popular sports for EU-citizens: through small but far-reaching popular policy projects such as the EUSB, sport can make a remarkable contribution to an EU-identity, notably popular sports. Due to the EU-identity blueprint, composed of seven identity markers, its positive impact and its consistence have been demonstrated. The EUSB has to power to encourage the foster the perception of *We are Europe*[547], which is unshirkably necessary.

Jean Monnet once said: "People only accept change in necessity and see necessity only in crisis." It cannot be denied that the EU's solidarity and coherence has been tested ever since it was founded, but particularly in the past few years. But the world has certainly noticed that the EU has stood together and will stand together in order to assure its own as well as its member states' viability. This necessity demands every EU-citizen's willingness to venture into the project of the EU, to be part of it, and to partake in the generation of an EU-identity. Simply stated, it is a *bare necessity*.

---

[541] Cf. **Körber**, Kurt A., Bergedorfer Gesprächskreis, pp. 49 f.
[542] **Risse**, Thomas, A Community of Europeans?, p. 13.
[543] Cf. **Schmitt-Egner**, Peter, Europäische Identität, p. 57.
[544] **Checkel**, Jeffrey T., **Katzenstein**, Peter J., Conclusion, p. 217.
[545] **McCormick**, John, Understanding the European Union, p. 32.
[546] Cf. **Tokarski**, Walter, Europa in Bewegung, p. 5.
[547] Cf. **Pagel**, Christoph, Festakt zum Tag der Deutschen Einheit.

Bibliography

Amt für amtliche Veröffentlichungen der Europäischen Gemeinschaften, Vertrag über eine Verfassung für Europa, Brüssel 2005.

Arter, David, The Politics of European Integration in the Twentieth Century, Cambridge 1993.

Berting, Jan, **Braak**, Hans van de, L'identité culturelle de la "Grande Europe" : mythe ou réalité, in : **Viallain-Gandossi**, Christiane, **Bochmann**, Klaus, **Metzeltin**, Michel, **Schäffner**, Christina (Eds.), Le concept de l'Europe dans le processus de la CSCE, Tübingen 1990.

Béthouart, Bruno, L'identité européenne chez les démocrates-chrétiens : conviction, évolution, in : **Villain-Gandossi**, Christiane (Ed.), L'Europe à la recherche de son identité, Paris 2002.

Bifulco, Marco, In search of an identity for Europe, Bonn 1998.

Bohne, Eberhard, EU and US Security Strategies from the Perspective of National and European Identities, Speyer 2006.

Borchardt, Klaus-Dieter, Das ABC des Rechts der Europäischen Union, Luxemburg 2010.

Bröskamp, Bernd, Glokalisierte Körper – Sport, Habitus und transnationale soziale Räume, in: **Blecking**, Diethelm, **Gieß-Stüber**, Petra (Eds..), Sport bewegt Europa. Beiträge zur interkulturellen Verständigung, Baltmannsweiler 2006.

Bruter, Michael, Citizens of Europe? The Emerge of a Mass European Identity, Houndmills 2005.

Calhoun, Craig, The Virtues of Inconsistency: Identity and Plurality in the Conceptualization of Europe, in: **Cederman**, Lars-Erik (Ed.), Constructing Europe's Identity. The external dimension, Boulder, CO 2001.

Cederman, Lars-Erik, Exclusion Versus Dilution: Real or Imagined Trade-Off, in: **Cederman**, Lars-Erik (Ed.), Constructing Europe's Identity. The external dimension, Boulder, CO 2001.

Checkel, Jeffrey T., **Katzenstein**, Peter J., The politicization of European identities, in: **Checkel**, Jeffrey T., **Katzenstein**, Peter J. (Eds.), European Identity, Cambridge 2009.

Cohn-Bendit, Daniel, **Verhofstadt**, Guy, Für Europa! Ein Manifest, Antwerpen 2012.

Czarny, Raphaël, Existe-t-il und identité européenne ?, im Internet unter : http://lyc-sevres.ac-versailles.fr/eee.eu08rcz.170408.pdf, [online] 05.01.2013.

Danckert, Peter, Kraftmaschine Parlament. Der Sportausschuss und die Sportpolitik des Bundes, Aachen 2009.

Darnstädt, Thomas , **Schult**, Christoph, **Zuber**, Helene, **Citizens of the EU.** How to Forge a Common European Identity, im Internet unter:

http://www.spiegel.de/international/europe/citizens-of-the-eu-how-to-forge-a-common-european-identity-a-800775.html, [online] 05.01.2013.

Darnstädt, Thomas, **Schult**, Christoph, **Zuber**, Helene, The Great Leap Forward. In Search of a United Europe, im Internet unter: http://www.spiegel.de/international/europe/the-great-leap-forward-in-search-of-a-united-europe-a-799292.html, [online] 05.01.2013.

Datler, Georg, Europäische Identität jenseits der Demos-Fiktion, Aus Politik und Zeitgeschichte, 2012 (4), pp. 57-61.

Daun, Åke, Cultural Diversity, in: **Daun**, Åke, **Jansson**, Sören (Eds.), Europeans. Essays on Culture and Identity, Lund 1999.

Dienel, Christiane, **Overkämping**, Sabine, Der Vertrag von Lissabon und die europäische Sozialpolitik, in: **Leiße**, Olaf (Ed.), Die Europäische Union nach dem Vertrag von Lissabon, Wiesbaden 2010.

Dominguez, Roberto, **Royo**, Sebastián, The Study of the European Integration Process in the United States, in: European Political Science, 2012 (3), pp. 285-308.

Dumont, Jacques, Le sport, vecteur d'intégration ? 1952, première tournée en Europe d'une équipe guadeloupéenne, in : **Villain-Gandossi**, Christiane (Ed.), L'Europe à la recherche de son identité, Paris 2002.

Enzensberger, Hans Magnus, Sanftes Monster Brüssel oder die Entmündigung Europas, Berlin 2011.

Europäische Kommission, Die Europäische Union und der Sport, Brüssel 1996.

Europäische Kommission, Mitteilung zum Sport (2011). Entwicklung der europäischen Dimension des Sports, Brüssel 2011.

Europäische Kommission, Weißbuch Sport, Brüssel 2007.

European Commission, White Paper on Sport, Brussels 2007.

Everling, Ulrich, Bindung und Rahmen: Recht und Integration, in: **Weidenfeld**, Werner (Ed.), Die Identität Europas, München 1985.

Flesch, Colette, Sport und Europäische Gemeinschaft aus Sicht der EG-Kommission, in: **Rydzy-Götz**, Marlis (Ed.), Die Europäische Gemeinschaft und der Sport, Frankfurt a.M. 1992.

Fligstein, Neil, Who are the Europeans and how does this matter for politics?, in: **Checkel**, Jeffrey T., **Katzenstein**, Peter J. (Eds.), European Identity, Cambridge 2009.

García, Borja, The Governance of European Sport, in: **Dine**, Philip, **Crosson**, Seán (Eds.), Sport, Representation and Evolving Identities in Europe, Oxford 2010.

Göler, Daniel, Die Grenzen des "Cost-of-Non-Europe"-Narrativs: Anmerkungen zur Sinnstiftung der Europäischen Integration, in: integration, 2012 (2), pp. 129-135.

Góra, Magdalena, **Mach**, Zdzisław, Democracy and Identity in Europe after Enlargment, in: **Góra**, Magdalena, **Mach**, Zdzisław, **Zielińska**, Katarzyna (Eds.), Collective Identity and Democracy in the Enlarging Europe, Frankfurt a.m. 2012.

Gruner, Wolf D., **Woyke**, Wichard, Europa-Lexikon. Länder – Politik – Institutionen, München 2004.

Guisan, Catherine, A political theory of identity in European integration. Memory and policies, London 2012.

Hänsch, Klaus, Perspektiven der europäischen Integration, in: **Leiße**, Olaf (Ed.), Die Europäische Union nach dem Vertrag von Lissabon, Wiesbaden 2010.

Hansen, Hans, Europa wächst zusammen, in: **Rydzy-Götz**, Marlis (Ed.), Die Europäische Gemeinschaft und der Sport, Frankfurt a.m. 1992.

Hapke, Yvonne, Identity and Integration in Europe. Personal Security and the Ties of Migrants and Majority Populations to their country, München 2009.

Heine, Peter, Islam in Europa als Problem einer europäischen Identität, in: **Kutz**, Martin, **Weyland**, Petra (Eds.), Europäische Identität? Versuch, kulturelle Aspekte eines Phantoms zu beschreiben, Bremen 2000.

Heisbourg, François, Restructuring European Security, in: **Weidendfeld**, Werner, **Janning**, Josef (Eds.), Global Responsibilities: Europe in Tomorrow's World, Gütersloh 1991.

Herz, Dietmar, **Jetzlsperger**, Christian, Die Europäische Union, München 2008.

Hick, Alan, Die Europäische Bewegung, in: **Loth**, Wilfried (Ed.), Die Anfänge der Europäischen Integration 1945-1950, Bonn 1990.

Hix, Simon, The Study of the European Community: The Challenge to Comparative Politics, in: **Nelsen**, Brent F., **Stubb**, Alexander C-G. (Eds.), The European Union, Boulder, CO 1994.

Hollaschke, Gerhard, Die EG-Integration zwischen Anpassung und Veränderung. Demokratietheoretische Überlegungen und institutionelle Reformen, in: **Strübel**, Michael (Ed.), Wohin treibt Europa? Der EG-Binnenmarkt und das Gemeinsame Europäische Haus, Marburg 1990.

Hooghe, Marc, Does Multi-level governance Reduce the Need for National Government?, in: European Political Science, 2012 (1), pp. 90-95.

Huysmans, Jef, European Identity and Migration Policies, in: **Cederman**, Lars-Erik (Ed.), Constructing Europe's Identity. The external dimension, Boulder, CO 2001.

Jacobs, Dirk, **Maier**, Robert, European Identity: construct, fact, fiction, in: **Gastelaars**, Marja, **Ruijter**, Arie de (Eds.), A United Europe. The Quest for a Multifaceted Identity, Maastricht 1998.

Janz, Louis, Die Geschichte der europäischen Einigung nach den Zweiten Weltkrieg, in: **Weidenfeld**, Werner (Eds.), Die Identität Europas, München 1985.

Katzenstein, Peter J., **Checkel**, Jeffrey T., Conclusion – European identity in context, in: **Checkel**, Jeffrey T., **Katzenstein**, Peter J. (Eds.), European Identity, Cambridge 2009.

Keltek, Tayfun, Sport als Mittel zur Integration, in: **Blecking**, Diethelm, **Gieß-Stüber**, Petra (Eds.), Sport bewegt Europa. Beiträge zur interkulturellen Verständigung, Baltmanns-weiler 2006.

Kepper, Christophe de, Die Europäische Union und der Sport, in: **Schimke**, Martin (Ed.), Sport in der Europäischen Union, Heidelberg 1996.

Kielmannsegg, Peter Graf, Integration und Demokratie, in: **Jachtenfuchs**, Markus, **Kohler-Koch**, Beate (Eds.), Europäische Integration, Opladen 2003.

Kohlhase, Norbert, Strategien der Europapolitik, in: **Weidenfeld**, Werner (Ed.), Die Identität Europas, München 1985.

Kommission der Europäischen Gemeinschaften, Europäische Identität: im Symbol, im Sport…, Stichwort Europa, 1987 (6).

Körber, Kurt A., Bergedorfer Gesprächskreis. Europa neu begründen. Kulturelle Dimensionen im Integrations- und Erweiterungsprozess, Hamburg 2003.

Küchenmeister, Daniel, **Schneider**, Thomas, Sport ist Teilhabe, Aus Politik und Zeitgeschichte, 2011 (16-19), pp. 3-8.

Kunzmann, Bernd, Europa 2012, Landau/Pfalz 2012.

Kutz, Martin, Zentrum und Peripherie, oder: Über den Zusammenhang von kultureller und wirtschaftlicher Dynamik Europas in Geschichte und Gegenwart, in: **Kutz**, Martin, **Weyland**, Petra (Eds.), Europäische Identität? Versuch, kulturelle Aspekte eines Phantoms zu beschreiben, Bremen 2000.

Landais, Joël, Identité nationale et identité européenne, im Internet unter : http://www.sauvonsleurope.eu/identite-nationale-et-identite-europeenne/, [online] 05.01.2013.

Lichtenstein, Dennis, Auf der Suche nach Europa: Identitätskonstruktionen und das integrative Potential von Identitätskrisen, in: **bpb magazin**, 01.03.2012, pp. 4-7.

Linklater, Andrew, A European Civilizing Process, in: **Hill**, Christopher, **Smith**, Michael (Eds.), International Relations and the European Union, New York, NY 2005.

Markovits, Andrei S., Sport: Motor und Impulssystem für Emanzipation und Diskriminierung, Wien 2011.

McCormick, John, Understanding the European Union. A Concise Introduction, New York, NY 2011.

Meyer, Thomas, Die Identität Europas, Frankfurt/Main 2004.

Mitchell, Mark, **Russell**, Dave, Immigration, citizenship and the nation-state in the new Europa, in: **Jenkins**, Brian, **Spyros**, A. Sofos (Eds.), Nation and Identity in Contemporary Europe, London 1996.

Muschg, Adolf, Was ist europäisch ?, Bonn 2005.

Pagel, Christoph, Festakt zum Tag der Deutschen Einheit. Lammert fordert ein „Wir sind Europa", im Internet unter: http://www.focus.de/politik/deutschland/festakt-zum-tag-der-deutschen-einheit-in-muenchen-lammert-fordert-ein-wir-sind-europa_aid_831691.html, [online] 05.01.2013.

Parkhalina, Tatyana, Europe. The concept of a »common European home« , in : **Viallain-Gandossi**, Christiane, **Bochmann**, Klaus, **Metzeltin**, Michel, **Schäffner**, Christina (Eds.), Le concept de l'Europe dans le processus de la CSCE, Tübingen 1990.

Richter, Christiane, Konzepte für den Schulsport in Europa. Bewegung, Sport und Gesundheit, Aachen 2006.

Riordan, James, **Krüger**, Arnd, **Terret**, Thierry, Histoire du Sport en Europe, Paris 2004.

Risse, Thomas, A Community of Europeans? Transnational Identities and Public Spheres, Ithaka, NY 2010.

Schäfers, Bernhard, Sozialstruktur und sozialer Wandel in Deutschland, Stuttgart 2002.

Schimmelpfennig, Frank, Zwischen Neo- und Postfunktionalismus: Die Integrationstheorien und die Eurokrise, in: Politische Vierteljahreszeitschrift, 2012 (3), pp. 394-413.

Schmale, Wolfgang, Geschichte und Zukunft der Europäischen Identität, Bonn 2010.

Schmitt-Egner, Peter, Europäische Identität. Ein konzeptioneller Leitfaden zu ihrer Erforschung und Nutzung, Baden-Baden 2012.

Schubotz, Dirk, **Svašek**, Maruška, **Miller**, Robert, **Domecka**, Markieta, Into and Out of Europe: Dynamic Insider/Outsider Perspectives, in: **Miller**, Robert, **Day**, Graham (Eds.), The Evolution of European Identities. Biographical approaches, Basingstoke 2012.

Seidl-Hohenveldern, Ignaz, Fragen zu Großeuropa, in: **Seidl-Hohenveldern**, Ignaz (Ed.), Auf dem Weg nach Europa – Fragen zur europäischen Integration, Köln 1991.

Singer, Otto, Sportpolitik der Europäischen Union nach dem Lissabon-Vertrag, http://www.bundestag.de/dokumente/analysen/2010/Sportpolitik_EU.pdf, [online] 05.01.2013.

Stelter, Reinhard, Du bist wie dein Sport. Studien zur Entwicklung von Selbstkonzept und Identität, Schorndorf 1996.

Szyszko, Agata, Die kulturelle Identität Europas als ideen- und begriffsgeschichtliches Konzept, in: **Birk**, Eberhard (Ed.), Aspekte einer europäischen Identität, Fürstenfeldbruck 2004.

Take, Ingo, Weltgesellschaft und Globalisierung, in: **Schieder**, Siegfried, **Spindler** Manuela (Eds.), Theorien der Internationalen Beziehungen, Opladen 2010.

Thatcher, Margaret, A Family of Nations, in: **Nelsen**, Brent F., **Stubb**, Alexander C-G. (Eds.), The European Union, Boulder, CO 1994.

Tokarski, Walter, Europa in Bewegung – Der Sport im „Europa der Bürger" gewinnt Konturen, in: **Tokarski**, Walter, **Petry**, Karen, **Schulz**, Norbert (Eds.), Brennpunkte der Sportwissenschaft. Sport im „Europa der Bürger". Neue Beiträge zum Zusammenwachsen des Sports im Europäischen Binnenmarkt, 1994 (1), pp. 3-7.

Tokarski, Walter, **Steinbach**, Dirk, Spuren. Sportpolitik und Sportstrukturen in der Europäischen Union, Aachen 2001.

Toussaint, Thomas, Identité européenne: la face cachée de la crise, http://www.lemonde.fr/idees/article/2012/07/18/identite-europeenne-la-face-cachee-de-la-crise_1734603_3232.html, [online] 05.01.2013.

Villain-Gandossi, Christiane, **Berting**, Jan, L'Europe, loin de la fin de l'histoire, in : **Villain-Gandossi**, Christiane (Ed.), L'Europe à la recherche de son identité, Paris 2002.

Vogt, Ludgera, Das Kapital der Bürger. Theorie und Praxis zivilgesellschaftlichen Engagements, Frankfurt/Main 2005.

Wæver, Ole, Discursive Approaches, in: **Wiener**, Antje, **Diez** Thomas (Eds.), European Integration Theory, Oxford 2009.

Wæver, Ole, **Kelstrup**, Morten, Europe and its nations: political and cultural identities, in: **Wæver**, Ole, **Buzan**, Barry, **Kelstrup**, Morten, **Lemaitre**, Pierre (Eds.), Identity, Migration and the New Security Agenda in Europe, London 1993.

Wagner, Hartmut, Bezugspunkte europäischer Identität, Berlin 2006.

Weidendfeld, Werner, **Janning**, Josef, After 1989: The Emerge of a new Europe, in: **Weidendfeld**, Werner, **Janning**, Josef (Eds.), Global Responsibilities: Europe in Tomorrow's World, Gütersloh 1991.

Weidenfeld, Werner, Europa im Umbruch: Perspektiven einer neuen Ordnung des Kontinents, in: **Weidenfeld**, Werner, **Stützle**, Walther (Eds.), Abschied von der alten Ordnung: Europas neue Sicherheit, Gütersloh 1990.

Weidenfeld, Werner, **Piepenschneider**, Melanie, Junge Generation und Europäische Einigung. Einstellungen – Wünsche – Perspektiven, Bonn 1990.

Weidenfeld, Werner, **Turek**, Jürgen, Wie Zukunft entsteht. Größere Risiken – weniger Sicherheit – neue Chancen, München 2002.

Westerwelle, Guido, Der Wert Europas: Vier Thesen zum Zukunftsprojekt Europa, in: integration, 2012 (2), pp. 90-93.

Wilke, Kurt, „Sportstudenten auf Achse in Europa" – Europäischer Studentenaustausch, in: **Tokarski**, Walter, **Petry**, Karen, **Schulz**, Norbert (Eds.), Brennpunkte der Sportwissenschaft. Sport im „Europa der Bürger". Neue Beiträge zum Zusammenwachsen des Sports im Europäischen Binnenmarkt, 1994 (1), pp. 8-23.